MEAN MACHINES
SPACECRAFT

TIM FURNISS

Raintree

www.raintreepublishers.co.uk
Visit our website to find out more information about **Raintree** books.

To order:
☎ Phone 44 (0) 1865 888113
▤ Send a fax to 44 (0) 1865 314091
▯ Visit the Raintree Bookshop at **www.raintreepublishers.co.uk** to browse our catalogue and order online.

First published in Great Britain by
Raintree, Halley Court,
Jordan Hill, Oxford OX2 8EJ,
part of Harcourt Education.
Raintree is a registered trademark of
Harcourt Education Ltd.

Produced for Raintree
by Discovery Books Ltd

Editorial: Diyan Leake and Carol Usher
Design: Michelle Lisseter and Keith Williams
Illustrations: Peter Bull and Stefan Chabluk
Picture research: Rachel Tisdale
Production: Jonathan Smith

Originated by Repro Multi Warna
Printed and bound in Hong Kong, China
by South China Printing Company

ISBN 1 844 43173 8
09 08 07 06 05
10 9 8 7 6 5 4 3 2 1

British Library Cataloguing in Publication Data
Furniss, Tim
Spacecraft – (Mean Machines)
I. Title
629.4'7
A full catalogue record for this book is available from
the British Library.

629.47

Acknowledgements
Corbis: pp. 6–7 (Hulton-Deutsch Collection); 22 (l)
(Bettmann), 27 (r), 34–35 & title page (NASA, 1996),
40–41, 44 (l) (Stocktrek), 48 (t) (Roger Ressmeyer) 54
(b) (Reuters); 55 (Jim Sugar), 56–57; Corbis Sygma:
pp. 32–33 (Alain Nogues); Genesis Space Photo
Library: pp. 4–5, 5 (t), 5 (m), 5 (b), 7 (b), 13, 15 (r), 16
(t), 16–17 (Steve Liss), 18 (l), 19, 20, 21, 22 (r), 24,
28, 30, 31, 32 (t), 33 (t), 36–37, 37 (t), 38, 39 (t), 39
(b), 44 (r), 48–49, 50, 54 (t), 57, 60, 61; NASA: pp.
12, 14–15, 17 (r), 23, 25, 26, 27 (l), 29, 34 (l), 35 (r),
40, 42 (l), 42–43, 43 (r), 45, 46, 47 (l), 47 (r), 49 (t),
51 (b), 52 (l), 52–53, 53 (t), 56; Novosti Photo
Library: pp. 9 (l), 9 (r), 10 (l), 10–11, 11 (r), 14 (l),
18 (r), 51 (t).

Cover photograph of *Atlantis* reproduced with
permission of Corbis (Stocktrek)

The publishers would like to thank Chris Welch for
his assistance in the preparation of this book

Every effort has been made to contact copyright
holders of any material reproduced in this book.
Any omissions will be rectified in subsequent printings
if notice is given to the publishers.

Disclaimer

CONTENTS

Any words appearing in the text in bold, **like this,** are explained in the Glossary. You can also look out for them in the Up To Speed box at the bottom of each page.

THE FINAL FRONTIER

The inky darkness goes on forever. The stars twinkle over vast distances. How many distant worlds are there in space? What are they like? Every person must look into the sky, ask questions like these and wonder…

DISTANT DREAM

Since the beginning of time, humans have dreamed of travelling into space. Those dreams only came true when people built spacecraft. Just imagine such a vehicle. To travel through the Earth's **atmosphere** and escape **gravity** it would have to travel at a terrific speed.

'THAT'S ONE SMALL STEP FOR MAN, ONE GIANT LEAP FOR MANKIND.'

These words were spoken by Neil Armstrong in July 1969, as he became the first human to walk on the surface of the Moon.

atmosphere   gases, liquids and solids that surround a planet
gravity   force of a large body, like Earth, on smaller objects

BURNING UP

Rushing back to Earth through the atmosphere, the heat would be incredible. The spacecraft would have to resist temperatures of 7000 °Celsius. Spacecraft are the most amazing vehicles.

SPACE AGE

In 1957, a **rocket** from the former Soviet Union, (now Russia), travelled into space at a speed of 28,000 kilometres (17,500 miles) per hour. It launched a **satellite** called *Sputnik 1*. This followed a curved path around the Earth. The Space Age had begun.

Since then spacecraft have taken people to the Moon. They have collected information about the planets. Humans have built stations in space and spacecraft have ferried people from Earth and back. Soon even ordinary people might travel into space.

This is the Space Shuttle *Endeavour*, flying above the Earth.

FIND OUT LATER...

*How is this **astronaut** getting around?*

What is this vehicle doing?

Which spacecraft is this rocket launching?

rocket   machine that gives a spacecraft the speed it needs to reach space
satellite   object that goes around a much larger body, like Earth, in space

ROCKET SCIENCE

How can you get a **rocket** to leave Earth's **gravity** and enter an **orbit** around Earth? A Russian schoolteacher called Konstantin Tsiolkovsky worked on this problem all his life. In 1903, he designed a rocket engine. Tsiolkovsky worked out how the rocket could enter space. This rocket would have to travel at a speed of 28,800 kilometres (18,000 miles) per hour.

HOW COLD IS THAT?

Liquid oxygen has to be extremely cold to stay liquid. The oxygen has to be kept at below −183 °Celsius.

TECH TALK

When the **exhaust** gases leave an engine's nozzle at high speed you get a huge force. This is called **thrust**.

huge force called thrust in opposite direction to gases

fuel and oxygen are burned

hot gases pass out of nozzle at high speed

A German V2 missile on display.

UP TO SPEED exhaust   waste gases from an engine
missile   rocket with a warhead

NOT HIGH ENOUGH

Before the Soviets could put a rocket into space, a scientist in the USA, Robert Goddard, fired the first liquid-fuelled rocket on 16 March 1926. The fuel was kerosene with liquid oxygen. The rocket flew to a height of 56 metres (184 feet) in 2.6 seconds. This was a big achievement but it did not reach space!

NEARLY THERE

Scientists continued to work on rockets, especially during World War II. One of the German V2 **missiles** reached a height of 80 kilometres (50 miles). Both the Soviet Union and the USA used the **technology** of the V2 to develop their first space rockets. Both countries wanted to reach space first and to put a **satellite** into orbit around the Earth. Then people could start to explore space!

A NEW TOWN IS BORN

The USA launched V2 rockets from White Sands, New Mexico. However, on 24 July 1950 a V2 or Bumper took off from a strip of sand on the Atlantic coast of Florida. It was called Cape Canaveral. This place is now world famous.

orbit   curved path followed by something around a large object in space
technology   use of science

SPUTNIK

Bleep, bleep … these sounds were heard all over the world. They were from outer space. The Space Age had begun, but how?

On 4 October 1957 the Soviet Union launched a **rocket**. It travelled fast enough to escape the Earth's **gravity**. When the rocket released a **satellite** it was not pulled back to the Earth by gravity. Instead it followed a curved path around the Earth. The satellite was called *Sputnik 1*. It was a **sphere** 60 centimetres (2 feet) in **diameter** and it had four radio aerials.

SPUTNIK 1'S ORBIT

Sputnik 1 orbited the Earth at a speed of 8 kilometres (5 miles) per second. One orbit took 1 hour and 36 minutes.

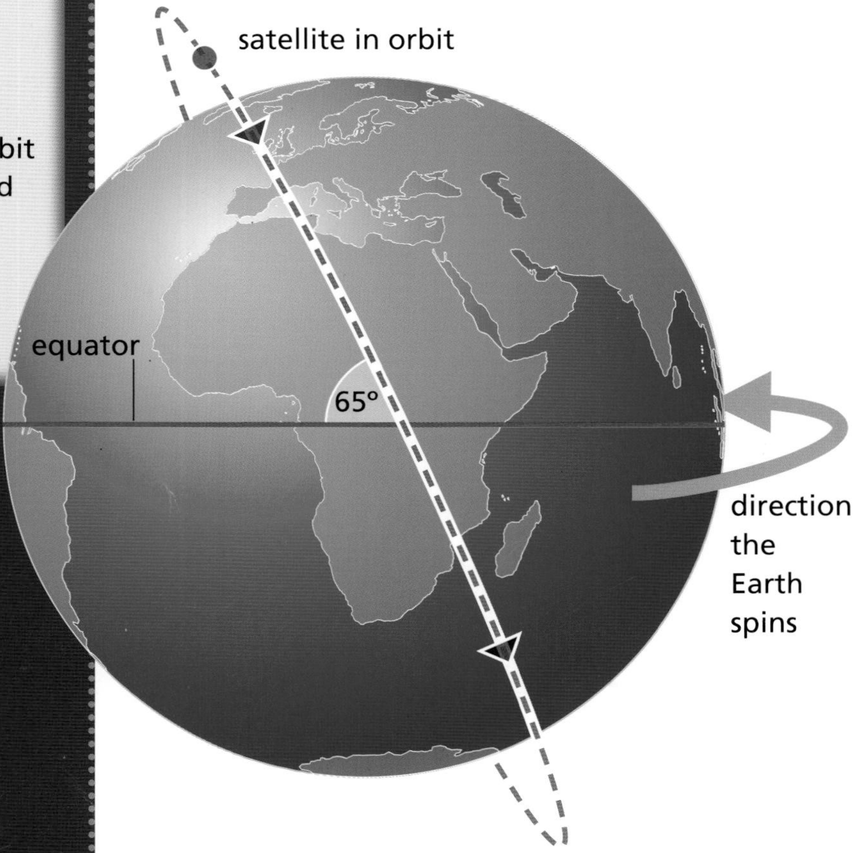

satellite in orbit

equator

65°

direction the Earth spins

diameter   distance from one side of a circle to another through the centre

The 84-kilogram *Sputnik 1* satellite.

Laika, the dog, in the satellite, *Sputnik 2*.

THE SPACE RACE

The launch of the satellite caused a shock in the western world. Most people thought the USA would reach space first because they had the better **technology**. A competition started between the two **super powers** of that time, the USA and the Soviet Union. It became known as the Space Race.

Then the Soviet Union launched another satellite, *Sputnik 2*, on 3 November 1957. This flew the first living creature into **orbit**. It was a dog called Laika.

The USA launched its first satellite on 31 January 1958. *Explorer 1* was a pencil-shaped craft. It had a **mass** of only 13 kilograms.

THE UNSUNG HEROES

Many animals went into space. A monkey, called Albert, is the first one we know about. He flew in a converted V2 rocket launched by the USA in 1948. Sadly, he died when the parachute on the **capsule** did not open.

FIRST PEOPLE IN SPACE

Just imagine being the first person to go into space. You might be extremely frightened and very excited about what would happen. A Russian, called Yuri Gagarin, had that honour in 1961. Inside a spacecraft called *Vostok 1* he made one **orbit** of the Earth. This took 1 hour and 48 minutes.

NOT REALLY THE FIRST

For a flight to be a record the **crew** has to be on the craft when the spacecraft lands. Yuri Gagarin (below) parachuted out of *Vostok 1* before it landed. His flight was not really the first official human spaceflight. But it was historic!

NO CONTROL

Vostok 1 had a tiny, ball-shaped flight cabin. It was only 2.3 metres (8 feet) in **diameter**. This was attached to an instrument unit. The instrument unit provided services like oxygen and included the retro-rocket. Gagarin had no actual control over the spacecraft. A **rocket** launched *Vostok 1* into its orbit. Only its special shape kept it on its flight path.

TECH TALK

A retro-rocket is a small rocket attached to the spacecraft. This is fired to slow the spacecraft down, so it can then orbit.

atmosphere   gases, liquids and solids that surround a planet
friction   when one object rubs against another. This causes heat.

RETURN TO EARTH

The flight cabin was the only part of the spacecraft to return to Earth. The spacecraft **re-entered** the Earth's **atmosphere** at a speed of 28,200 kilometres (17,500 miles) per hour. The **friction** against the atmosphere made the spacecraft very hot. The flight cabin's heat shield stopped it burning up. Gagarin ejected from the flight cabin and parachuted to safety before *Vostok 1* made a very hard landing.

FIRST WOMAN IN SPACE

Valentina Tereshkova (below) flew aboard *Vostok 6* in June 1963. Sadly, she felt space sick most of the time.

The rocket containing *Vostok 1* is **erected** on the launch pad.

➤➤➤➤➤➤➤➤➤➤➤
Find out more about space sickness on page 29.

orbit curved path followed by something around a large object in space
re-entry high-speed return of a space vehicle through the Earth's atmosphere

The USA's *Freedom 7* is launched on a Redstone rocket.

MERCURY GOES UP

The USA's human space flight programme started with Project Mercury in May 1961. The Mercury **capsule** was shaped like a cone and was very small. It was 2.7 metres (9 feet) high and 1.85 metres (6 feet) wide at the base. It could only take one person. The **astronaut** had to squeeze through a small hatch to get into the tiny cabin. He was then strapped on to a couch.

GOING LIVE

The Soviet Vostok flights in the early 1960s were made in secret. The Soviets only announced them when their people were in space. The USA **broadcast** live television and radio programmes about Project Mercury. People all over the world saw and heard the launches as they took place.

IN CONTROL

The control panels were more advanced on the Mercury spacecraft than the Vostok spacecraft. The astronaut was able to steer the spacecraft up and down, round and round and sideways. The Mercury spacecraft could make landings too. It splashed down into the sea rather than on to the ground, under a single parachute.

TECH TALK

In the USA, people are awarded astronaut's 'wings' when they fly higher than 80 kilometres (50 miles) above the Earth.

astronaut   space traveller
broadcast   give out information on the radio or television

FIRST AMERICAN IN SPACE

Alan Shepard flew his Mercury capsule, *Freedom 7* on a **suborbital** flight, in May 1961. This took 15 minutes. He took off from Cape Canaveral and splashed down in the Atlantic Ocean. John Glenn, who became a national hero, made the first US flight in **orbit**, on 20 February 1962.

NO NEED FOR THE TOILET

Early astronauts ate special food. There was no need to go to the toilet because the body used all of this food and there was hardly any solid waste. Urine was collected in a bag in the spacesuit.

Alan Shepard is recovered by a helicopter after his splashdown in *Freedom 7*.

capsule   part of a spacecraft, which comes apart from the rest
suborbital   flight into space that does not go fast enough to go into orbit

MOON PREPARATION

The Soviets and the Americans both wanted to land a person on the Moon. There was a lot of work to do before they could. Two spacecraft would have to **rendezvous** (pronounced 'ron-day-voo') and then **dock**. Astronauts would have to **spacewalk** outside the spacecraft. They would have to stay in space for up to fourteen days.

The US agency, **NASA**, built a two-man craft called Gemini. Gemini was shaped like Mercury, but was bigger. It measured 5.5 metres (18 feet) long and had a base of 3 metres (10 feet). It was launched on a powerful *Titan 2* **missile rocket**. Two test flights were made without **crew** before *Gemini 3* flew in March 1965.

THE FIRST SPACEWALK

Alexei Leonov, from *Voshkod 2* was the first to spacewalk on 18 March 1965.

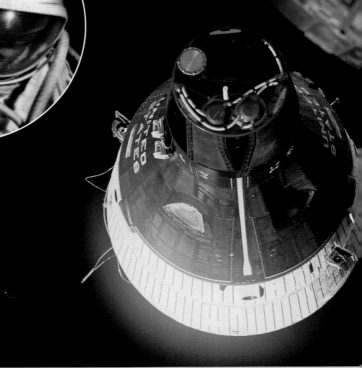

This is Alexei Leonov. He was spacewalking outside *Voshkod 2* for about 10 minutes.

dock   join up with another spacecraft in space
NASA   National Aeronautics and Space Agency

PRACTICE MAKES PERFECT

The USA's *Gemini 3* managed to move into a different **orbit**. On the *Gemini 4* mission, Edward White became the first American to spacewalk. *Gemini 7* stayed in space for fourteen days. It also came to within 30 centimetres (1 foot) of *Gemini 6*. *Gemini 8* made the first docking in March 1966.

The fast pace continued. Astronauts practised how to rendezvous and dock. More spacewalks were made and crews learned to work outside the spacecraft. The USA was ready for the Moon!

Find out more about Apollo missions on pages 20–25 and about spacewalking on page 31.

GOOD TRAINING

Pete Conrad (below) flew on *Gemini 5* and *11* and became the third man on the Moon on the *Apollo 12* mission. He later commanded the first *Skylab* mission in 1973.

Gemini 6 and *Gemini 7* make the first rendezvous in space.

rendezvous   get close to another spacecraft in orbit
spacewalk   move about outside the spacecraft in space

X-15 pilots from left to right: Joe Engle, Robert Rushworth, Jack McKay, Pete Knight, Milton Thompson and Bill Dana.

ROCKET PLANES

How do you think you could get into space? You might think you could fly there in an aeroplane. This is what the Americans thought in the 1940s and 50s. They used planes with **rocket** engines called rocket planes.

BREAKING THE SOUND BARRIER

In October 1947, pilot Chuck Yeager flew the X-1 rocket plane to a record speed of Mach 1.06. He became the first man to fly faster than the **speed of sound**. Milburn Apt became the first person to fly at Mach 3, in 1956, but was killed when his X-2 crashed.

TECH TALK

A Mach number tells us how many times faster the speed of a craft is compared to the speed of sound in air. Mach 6 is six times the speed of sound.

The record-breaking X-1 rocket plane.

altitude   height of something above sea level

X-15

Engineers designed a new, faster rocket plane, the X-15. The X-15 was a slick, needle-like rocket plane. Its first flight was on 8 June 1959. Like some of the other rocket planes, another plane carried the X-15 to a high **altitude** and then released it. The USA planned to launch the X-15 on top of a rocket and for it to reach space.

FASTER AND FASTER

On 17 July 1962, Robert White reached an **altitude** of 95 kilometres (59 miles). Twelve X-15 pilots flew to an altitude of 80 kilometres (50 miles) or more, gaining their **astronaut's** wings. Pete Knight flew an X-15 at a world record speed of Mach 6.70, in October 1967.

A TRAGIC END

In November 1967, pilot Mike Adams flew an X-15 into space, but lost control of the craft. It spiralled down to Earth at incredible speed. The craft broke apart and smashed into the Mojave Desert in California, USA.

The X-15 rocket plane being released from a B52 plane.

‹‹‹‹‹‹‹‹‹‹‹‹
Find out more about astronaut's wings on page 12.

speed of sound   speed at which sound waves travel

TO THE MOON

EARLY EXPLORATION

Before people could land on the Moon, scientists had to find out what the Moon was like. Spacecraft were sent to the Moon with no one on board. They were flown automatically.

RANGER 7

The 1.5-metre (5 feet) tall *Ranger 7* (below) took the first close look at the Moon's surface in 1964. It had six TV cameras. These took 4000 images as *Ranger 7* fell towards the Sea of Clouds at a speed of 9000 kilometres (5500 miles) per hour.

LUNA 2 AND 3

The first spacecraft to hit the Moon was a Soviet one, called *Luna 2*. It crashed at high speed near the Archimedes **crater** on 14 September 1959. A month later, *Luna 3* flew around the far side of the Moon.

The Soviet Union's Luna 3 was the first spacecraft to take pictures of the far side of the Moon.

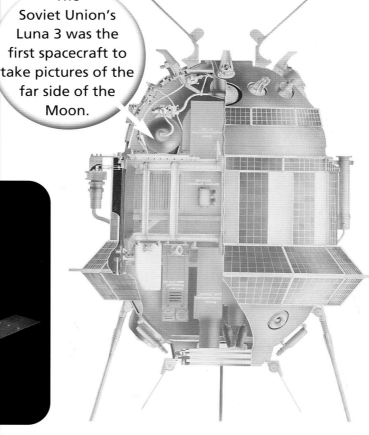

crater   large hollow, shaped like a bowl
plummet   fall very quickly

AN ORBIT AND A LANDING

The Soviet's *Luna 10* was the first spacecraft to **orbit** around the Moon. The USA made the first **rocket**-controlled soft landing in June 1966 with *Surveyor 1*.

Scientists found some sites where spacecraft could land safely. One site was on the Sea of Tranquillity. The race to the Moon was reaching its most exciting point.

SURVEYOR

The Surveyor (below) was 3 metres (10 feet) high and looked a bit like an insect with a heavy camera (weighing 7.3 kilograms). This took images of the surface. Some craft had a **robot** arm with a shovel. This dug up some moon soil.

rocket   machine that gives a spacecraft the speed it needs to reach space

SATURN 5

The aim of Project Apollo was to put people on the Moon. Everything about Project Apollo was big. It was a big challenge, big money and it had a huge **rocket**. This was called the *Saturn 5* and it was a monster booster.

The Saturns were **erected** on a mobile launch pad. It was rolled out slowly on huge tractors, called crawlers, to the launch area. When *Saturn 5* was launched, the ground shook like an earthquake, even at 5 kilometres (3 miles) away.

NOT MUCH LEFT

All that came back from the 112-metre (367-feet) high rocket and spacecraft was a **module** 3.7 metres (12 feet) high. It had three people aboard.

This is the launch of *Apollo 11* aboard a *Saturn 5* booster on 16 July 1969.

erect   build so that it is upright
gravity   force of a large body, like Earth, on smaller objects

The *Saturn 5* had five huge first-stage engines (left). Each engine gulped 13,620 kilograms (15 tons) of liquid oxygen and kerosene every second. The total load was 1.5 million litres (40 million gallons).

POWERFUL ENGINES

The *Saturn 5* was 112 metres (367 feet) tall. It had three powerful stages. The engines of each stage fired in turn to take the rocket into **orbit**. The time from Saturn's blast-off to reaching orbit was about 12 minutes. Later, the engine restarted. It sent Apollo towards the Moon fast enough to escape the pull of Earth's **gravity**.

APOLLO'S FLIGHT JOURNEY

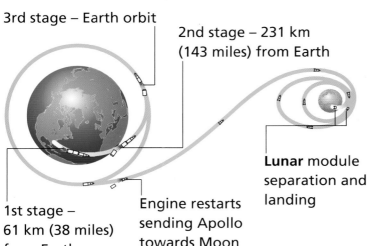

3rd stage – Earth orbit

2nd stage – 231 km (143 miles) from Earth

Apollo's flight from the Earth to the Moon. This is 384,000 kilometres (238,000 miles).

Lunar module separation and landing

1st stage – 61 km (38 miles) from Earth

Engine restarts sending Apollo towards Moon

lunar   about the moon
module   part of a spacecraft. It can exist by itself.

APOLLO MISSIONS

In 1968, Frank Borman, James Lovell and William Anders flew *Apollo 8* around the far side of the Moon. They were completely out of contact with the Earth then. Two more flights followed to test all the systems. One was in Earth **orbit** and another was in **lunar** orbit.

THE EAGLE HAS LANDED

Then came the historic *Apollo 11* mission. On 20 July 1969, the **module** *Eagle* landed on the Moon's 'Sea of Tranquillity'. Neil Armstrong was the first man to step on to the Moon. He was joined quickly by Buzz Aldrin. *Apollo 12* followed in November 1969. The **astronauts** Pete Conrad and Al Bean made two walks on the Moon's Ocean of Storms. They reached a **robot lander** called *Surveyor 3*, as planned.

The *Apollo 13* command module is recovered from the Pacific Ocean.

Here is a picture of Earth taken from the Moon by *Apollo 8*.

budget   amount of money put aside for a project
crew   people that operate the spacecraft

LUNAR MODULE

The Apollo spacecraft had a Command and Service Module (CSM) and a Lunar Module (LM). The CSM carried the three astronauts, the systems and a **rocket** engine. The LM had two parts. The **descent** stage had an engine for the landing on the Moon. The **ascent** stage was on top of the descent stage. It had an engine to take the astronauts back to the CSM. The descent stage was left on the Moon.

There were four more Apollo missions and many walks on the Moon. By 1972 it was clear the USA had beaten the Soviet Union in the Space Race. The USA lost interest and **budgets** were cut. Nobody has walked on the Moon since.

TRUE OR FALSE?

There is water on the Moon.

False. The 'seas' or 'oceans' are the smooth areas on the Moon. From the Earth they looked like oceans to early observers.

The *Apollo 11* lunar module and Buzz Aldrin, 20 July 1969.

◄ ◄ ◄ ◄ ◄ ◄ ◄ ◄ ◄ ◄ ◄ ◄
Find out more about the far side of the Moon and Surveyor on page 19.

lander part of the spacecraft that lands on the planet to be explored
robot machine that can carry out tasks without the help of people

OUT AND ABOUT

It is impossible to leave a spacecraft without protection. There is no air on the Moon. The temperature in the sunlight is 105 °Celsius and in darkness it is -155 °Celsius. There is deadly **radiation**. **Micrometeoroids** could hit you. Your blood would either boil or freeze, if you were not protected from this **environment**. You would die very quickly. Each Apollo moonwalker had a made-to-measure spacesuit for protection.

Astronaut John Young jumps on the Moon during the Apollo 16 mission.

TECH TALK

Mass is the measure of how much there is of something. It stays the same wherever it is. Weight depends on gravity. Something will weigh heavier on the Earth than on the Moon because gravity is greater on the Earth.

environment   conditions around you
mass   how much there is of something

MOON CAR

On the *Apollo 15–17* missions, the **astronauts** were able to travel further from the **Lunar Module** because they had a car, or **rover** This was called a Lunar Roving Vehicle (LRV). It was packed into the side of the Lunar Module. On the surface of the Moon it was converted into a two-seater moon car with four wire-mesh wheels.

The LRV had a **mass** of 208 kilograms and was 3 metres (10 feet) long. Two batteries powered it. The LRV could carry rocks and drive for many miles. It had a large aerial dish too. This allowed the astronauts to talk to people on Earth.

LUNAR ROVER

The fastest speed an LRV achieved was about 15 kilometres (9 miles) per hour. The first LRV on *Apollo 15* travelled a total of 17 kilometres.

micrometeoroid   particle of dust in space that travels very fast
radiation   energy, such as light and heat, that can travel through space

SPACE SHUTTLE

The Space Shuttle was supposed to fly into **orbit** every week. People thought that it would carry passengers and **cargo** to and from a space station regularly and cheaply. In fact each Space Shuttle journey costs about US $500 million and there are only about six flights a year. We still have a long way to go before flying into space will be like an airline service.

AN AMAZING MACHINE

Since 1981, the Space Shuttle orbiters *Columbia*, *Challenger*, *Discovery*, *Atlantis* and *Endeavour* have flown over 113 missions.

The Americans have carried out scientific experiments and built a space station in space. The Space Shuttle has put **satellites** and telescopes into space, repaired them and put them back again.

A launch of the Space Shuttle *Discovery* from one of the two launch pads at the Kennedy Space Centre, Florida.

◄◄◄◄◄◄◄◄◄◄◄◄◄◄
Find out more about liquid oxygen on page 6.

cargo   things that are carried on a vehicle, such as a satellite on a Space Shuttle

SPACE SHUTTLE PARTS

The Space Shuttle has an **orbiter**, **external** tank and solid **rocket** boosters. The orbiter is the section where the people are. The Space Shuttle normally carries seven people. This part of the Space Shuttle can be used again. It has a large area where all sorts of cargo, from space station parts to **telescopes** and cameras, are placed.

The external tank holds the liquid oxygen and liquid hydrogen for the orbiter's three main engines. The two solid rocket boosters use solid fuel. They provide extra power for the first two minutes of flight.

The Space Shuttle orbiter *Challenger*. Its **payload bay** is open and you can see its **robot** arm.

DISASTERS

Challenger exploded when it was launched, in January 1986. In February 2003, *Columbia* broke apart during its **re-entry**. These accidents killed fourteen **astronauts** altogether.

Challenger exploding. After this the Space Shuttle programme was halted until September 1988.

orbiter   part of a spacecraft that goes into orbit
telescope   instrument that uses mirrors and lenses to view distant objects

Astronaut
Susan Still floats
inside a Spacelab
laboratory on the
Space Shuttle
in 1997.

IN THE SHUTTLE

The main living area of the Space Shuttle is in the nose section of the **orbiter**. There are two floors. The upper deck is the **cockpit**, which has four seats. The mid-deck carries up to four more seats. This is also the experiment area, living room, kitchen, toilet and exercise room. Living on the Shuttle is like being on a camping trip. It is certainly not luxury, but the views are awesome.

PLAYING IN SPACE

In space there is no force holding you to the ground. This is called **zero-gravity**. People in space are weightless and can have great fun floating about.

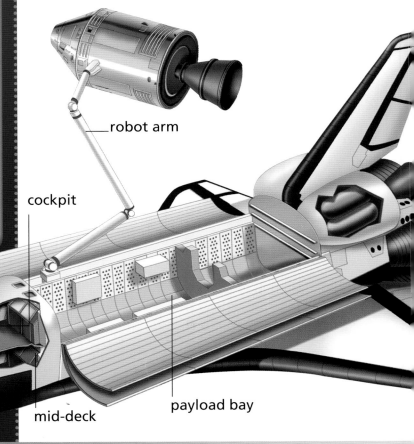

robot arm

cockpit

payload bay

mid-deck

DOWN BELOW

An airlock in the mid-deck leads into the **payload bay** and two **spacewalkers** can enter. The payload bay is inside the long **fuselage**. It carries the main **cargo** for the mission. The cargo might be a section of a space station, **satellites**, or a space **telescope**. Satellites can also be brought back and serviced in the payload bay. Although the payload bay is inside the long Space Shuttle fuselage, it is exposed to space when two doors open. The doors open like flaps along the whole length of the fuselage.

The **astronauts** can do jobs in the payload bay like repairing equipment and constructing the space station. A **robot** arm does some jobs. This is mounted in the payload bay, but the astronaut in the cockpit controls it.

Space Shuttle **crew** members are asleep in the lower mid-deck of the orbiter.

This diagram shows the layout of the Space Shuttle orbiter.

Find out more about satellites on pages 32–39.

payload bay area or space where most of the cargo is stored
spacewalk move about outside the spacecraft in space

ROBOT ARM

The Space Shuttle carries lots of equipment to do jobs in space. One very important piece of equipment is the Remote Manipulator System (RMS) or **robot** arm. The RMS works like a human arm. It is 15 metres (49 feet) long and has a shoulder, elbow, wrist and a grapple. The grapple is like a hand and can hold objects. To operate a RMS, the **astronaut** uses a hand controller to get the robot arm to hold on to **cargo,** tools or even a **spacewalker.** The RMS can carry and move large objects around the **payload bay** or transfer them to the space station.

A spacewalker is at the end of the Space Shuttle's Remote Manipulator System.

SPACEHAB

clamp   something that holds two parts together very tightly
EVA   Extra-Vehicular Activity, or activity outside the vehicle

SINGLE FLIGHT

A Manned Manoeuvring Unit (MMU) allows astronauts to move around in space.
A SAFER (Simplified Air for **EVA** Rescue) returns astronauts to the Space Shuttle if their **tethers** disconnect during a spacewalk.

Bruce McCandless was the first person to fly in space, using a Manned Manoeuvring Unit. This was in February 1984.

TAKING A SPACEWALK

Astronauts need special suits for spacewalking. These are called **Environmental** Mobility Units (EMUs). They are cooling and **ventilator** suits. A backpack provides oxygen and life-support systems. These can give an astronaut support on a spacewalk for about seven hours.

SPACESUIT

Spacesuits come in several sizes and have two main parts. The lower section is like a pair of trousers and is put on first. The upper section is put on next. A **clamp** on the waist joins the two parts together. Gloves and the helmet are clamped on too.

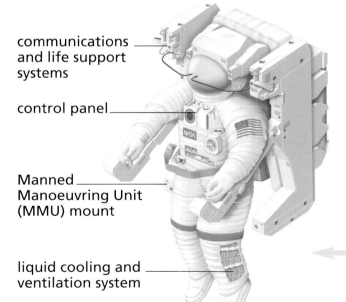

communications and life support systems

control panel

Manned Manoeuvring Unit (MMU) mount

liquid cooling and ventilation system

This diagram shows the different parts of a spacesuit.

tether   wire that attaches an astronaut to the spacecraft
ventilator   machine that gets air to flow into a small space, like a spacesuit

SATELLITES IN SPACE

This is a huge communications satellite built in the USA. It is providing services to Japan.

Many of the things we take for granted depend on special spacecraft called **satellites**. A typical communications satellite has a **mass** of about 5000 kilograms. It is like a small detached house. Satellites beam TV programmes around the world. Satellites also relay telephone calls, faxes, emails and the Internet all at the same time. The first communications satellite, *Telstar*, was launched in 1962. Since then, satellites have changed how we communicate beyond our wildest dreams.

ABOVE US ALL THE TIME!

Communications satellites move around the world at the same speed as the Earth **rotates**. This means the satellite is always above the same part of the Earth. It can give a service to the area it covers all of the time.

A satellite image showing sea winds across the Earth's oceans.

monitor   watch over something regularly
pollution   harmful substances in the environment

The European Space Agency's XMM X-ray **astronomical telescope**.

USEFUL INFORMATION

Satellites are in **orbit** around the Earth all the time. They **monitor** the weather and **environment** of the Earth. Satellites measure the Earth's **gravity**, the temperature of the sea, **pollution** and even wind speeds. Science satellites monitor the Earth's **radiation** belts.

Information from the satellites can help many industries. Knowing about the temperature of the seas helps the fishing industry. Exact measurements of the Earth's surface are very useful to road builders.

THE SUN'S POWER

Most satellites carry large solar panels. These convert sunlight into electricity and provide the satellite with power.

rotate   turn around an axis or central point
satellite   object that goes around a much larger body, like Earth, in space

TELESCOPE IN SPACE

Astronomers have always wanted to see further into the **universe**. The best way to do this is to place a **telescope** into space. Telescopes on the Earth cannot 'see' into space very well because of the **atmosphere**. However, in space the sky is clear.

HUBBLE SPACE TELESCOPE

Engineers built the Hubble Space Telescope (HST) to work outside the Earth's atmosphere, in space. The HST can see fifty times deeper into space than the most powerful telescope on Earth. The Space Shuttle put the HST into **orbit** in April 1990.

THE SPACE SHUTTLE AND THE HUBBLE SPACE TELESCOPE

Four Space Shuttle missions were flown to service the HST. After the *Columbia* disaster in 2003, further missions were cancelled.

A Space Shuttle **astronaut** is servicing the Hubble Space Telescope.

astronomer   person who studies stars and planets
galaxy   group of stars in space

A VIEW OF DEEP SPACE

The HST has completely changed astronomy. It has sent back spectacular images of the universe. These have fired the imagination of the whole world. We have seen pictures of huge spiral **galaxies** and the births and deaths of stars. The first image of a star, called Betelgeuse (pronounced 'beetle-juice'), was sent back to Earth during the 1990s. This star is nearly as big as our **solar system**.

TECH TALK

The Hubble Space Telescope has a **mass** of 11,600 kilograms (12¾ tons). It is 13 metres (42 feet) long and 4.2 metres (14 feet) in **diameter**.

BETELGEUSE (BEETLE-JUICE)

This star is 500 times larger than the Sun and 10,000 times brighter. It is the tenth-brightest star in the sky.

The Hubble Space Telescope took this picture of the giant star Betelgeuse.

SPY SATELLITES

A military **satellite** or spy satellite could see a football from over 400 kilometres (250 miles) up in space. Military satellites spy on the movement of troops and vehicles. They can easily detect a **missile** launch on the Earth.

These satellites fly around Earth in polar **orbits**. This means the satellites fly over the poles of the Earth. The satellites can take images in most parts of the world in a 24-hour period.

BIG BROTHER

Some satellites can listen to telephone calls and **monitor** other types of communications. These are called Electronic Intelligence Satellites or Elints. The huge receiving dishes are 100 metres (325 feet) in **diameter**.

POLAR ORBITS

Satellites in polar orbits 'view' most areas of the Earth during a day because they fly around the Earth seventeen times in 24 hours. The Earth only **rotates** beneath the satellite once in this time. Some weather satellites also use these types of orbit.

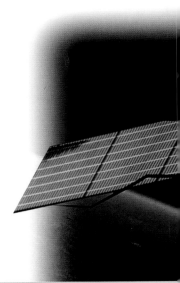

North Pole

Equator

direction the Earth spins

South Pole

path of satellite

ENEMY MOVEMENTS

American **reconnaissance** (pronounced 'rec-on-ess-ons') satellites send images straight into the National Reconnaissance Office in Washington DC, USA. Officials look at them very closely. They are searching for clues about enemy movements.

This picture of London was taken by a satellite. It can show objects as small as 1 metre (3 feet) in diameter. Spy satellites can see even closer.

FINDING YOUR WAY

The military services use **navigation** satellites for guiding aircraft or missiles to their targets. Today navigation satellites also help drivers of ordinary cars to find where they are going.

SPYING AT NIGHT

Some spy satellites have special sensors. These detect the body heat of a human being. This shows the position of people or animals. The sensors work at night, as well as in the day.

A US Navstar GPS navigation satellite orbits the Earth. You can see its pen-like radio aerial.

reconnaissance looking closely at an area, especially by the military

BIG BUSINESS

Fleets of **commercial** launch vehicles carry **satellites** into space as a business. Many **rockets** can carry up to three satellites at once.

MONSTER BOOSTERS

The largest rockets of all carry the huge communications satellites. The rockets place them into **orbits**, where the satellite stays above the same point on the Earth all the time. The major launchers are *Ariane 5*, *Atlas 5*, *Delta 4* and *Sea Launch*.

CROWDED SPACE

The USA and Russia both launch about twenty satellites every year. Altogether, Europe, India, Japan and China make about twenty launches in a year. Space is getting crowded and this could be a problem in the future.

The *Sea Launch Zenit 3SL* booster launches satellites from a floating offshore platform.

amplify   make a signal stronger
commercial   organizations that make money

ARIANE

The most famous launcher company is Arianespace. This European company uses the Ariane rocket. Ariane has a main central stage with one engine. This uses liquid oxygen and liquid hydrogen. The main stage also has two solid rocket boosters attached to it. These are very powerful rockets with solid fuel. These give a big boost early in the flight. Ariane only needs a smaller upper stage engine because of the two solid rocket boosters.

A Hot Bird European communications satellite being assembled in a factory.

ENORMOUS WINGS

A typical communications satellite has a wingspan of 60 metres (195 feet). They are equipped with about 50 transponders. Transponder units receive signals from the Earth, **amplify** them and send them to other parts of the Earth.

Ariane 5, on the pad, waiting for launch.

orbit   curved path followed by something around a large object in space

SPACE EXPLORATION

In just 27 years, between 1962 and 1989, spacecraft explored eight of the nine planets in the **solar system**. The only planet left is the distant Pluto.

VICIOUS VENUS

Venera 10 landed on Venus (right) in 1970 and sent information back to Earth for 65 minutes before the heat knocked it out. The temperature on the surface is 460 °Celsius and the **atmospheric pressure** is 92 times greater than the Earth's. It also rains sulphuric acid!

DESTINATION VENUS

Venus was the first planet to be explored. *Mariner 2* found out information about Venus in 1962. It is about the same size as the Earth and has a thick **atmosphere** of carbon dioxide cloud. This traps the heat from the Sun and makes Venus a very hot place indeed. Amazingly, some spacecraft landed on the surface of Venus and sent pictures back to Earth. The Soviet Union made the first landings with Venera craft, in 1970. The first colour images from the surface were sent back to Earth in 1981.

TECH TALK

Venus is quite a dark place – a bit like a very foggy day on Earth. This is because it has such a thick atmosphere.

atmosphere   gases, liquids and solids that surround a planet

MISSION MERCURY

A US spacecraft, *Mariner 10*, flew past Mercury three times in 1974–75. Mercury is the planet closest to the Sun and looks like the Moon. The temperature on Mercury is about 430 °Celsius. This is hot enough to melt lead. Other Mercury missions are planned in the next few years, including an **orbiter**.

GETTING CLOSE

Mariner 10 had a **mass** of 503 kilograms and was equipped with two cameras. These looked like the eyes of a huge insect. The craft flew to within 327 kilometres (203 miles) of the planet Mercury.

America's *Mariner 10* was the first spacecraft to explore the planet Mercury. Mercury is the closest planet to the Sun.

Is there life on Mars? If life on Mars is ever found, it will probably be very simple forms, like single cells or **microbes**.

MARINER

The first spacecraft to fly past Mars was *Mariner 4*, in 1965. It discovered the planet is covered in **craters**. Later spacecraft saw deep valleys, high mountains and volcanoes. The first spacecraft **orbited** Mars in 1971. It was called *Mariner 9*. *Viking 1* was the first craft to make a landing, in 1976.

MISSION END

The US rovers *Spirit* and *Opportunity* only worked for about six months. Too much dust built up on their solar panels and Mars had moved away from the Sun. The rovers were then not able to get enough power to move.

An artist's impression of one of the two Mars Exploration Rovers, / and *Opportunity*, travelling across the Martian surface.

This is a model of *Sojourner*, the Mars Pathfinder rover.

crater   large hollow, shaped like a bowl
microbe   tiny living thing that can be seen under a microscope

VIKING LANDS

The pictures taken by Viking showed a red-orangey coloured surface, with lots of rocks. It looked like a desert on the Earth. Scientists **analysed** samples of soil, but found no signs of life.

In 1997, the USA's *Mars Pathfinder* landed on Mars and used a **rover** for the first time. This was the *Sojourner*. It managed to move about 20 metres (65 feet) from *Pathfinder*.

MARS LANDING

The US rovers *Spirit* and *Opportunity* landed on Mars in January 2004. They analysed rocks and found ice. This shows there is water on Mars. This means there may also be life. The British **lander**, called *Beagle 2*, was supposed to land on 25 December 2003, but was lost.

TECH TALK

Most of the Martian **atmosphere** is carbon dioxide. There is a lot of dangerous **radiation** and the temperature often goes below −100 °Celsius at night.

Beagle 2 had a **mass** of only 33 kilograms (72$\frac{3}{4}$ pounds). One-third of this was scientific instruments.

This is what *Beagle 2* was supposed to look like on Mars.

radiation   energy, such as light and heat, that can travel through space
rover   space vehicle with wheels

PIONEER AND VOYAGER

Jupiter, Saturn, Uranus and Neptune are all further away from us than Mars. They are giant planets made of gas. These are more difficult to explore because they are so far away.

Pioneer 10 took the first close-up images of the clouds of Jupiter when it flew past in 1973. *Pioneer 11* was the first craft to explore Saturn in 1979. Images from *Pioneer 11* showed Saturn's rings close up. *Voyager 2* explored Uranus in 1986 and Neptune in 1989.

PIONEER 10

Pioneer 10 (shown in an artist's impression below) carries a plaque showing a man and a woman, and a map of the **solar system**. The map shows the path of the craft and the position of the Earth.

Here is an artist's impression of the *Voyager* spacecraft.

capsule   part of a spacecraft that comes apart from the rest
data   information or scientific measurements

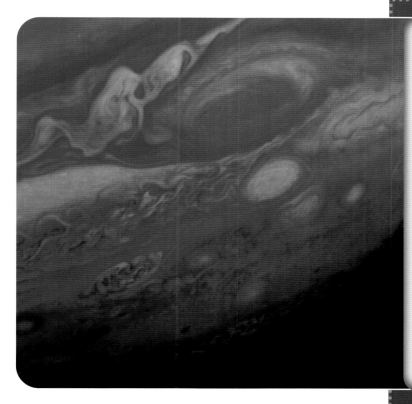

Galileo has taken close-up images of the Great Red Spot. This is a huge storm of poisonous gases in Jupiter's atmosphere. This storm could swallow up three Earths. The winds blow at a speed of more than 32,000 kilometres (20,000 miles) per hour.

GALILEO

Galileo was the first spacecraft to **orbit** Jupiter in 1995. It released a **capsule**. This plunged into the **turbulent atmosphere** and sent back **data**. *Galileo* took fantastic images of the main Jupiter moons, Io, Europa, Callisto and Ganymede. The spacecraft enters orbit around Saturn in 2004, sending a capsule to land on a moon, called Titan.

Another spacecraft will orbit Jupiter. This will take a much closer look at the volcanic moon Io and the icy, watery world of Europa. The first Pluto explorer is planned to reach the planet around 2016.

TECH TALK

The Jupiter moon, Io, is a world of **sulphur** volcanoes and lava. Volcanoes on the surface ooze liquid sulphur and spew out sulphur gases 300 kilometres (185 miles) into space.

sulphur   yellow, non-metal, chemical element
turbulent   moving fast in all directions

COMETS

The **solar system** contains comets and asteroids, as well as planets. Comets are huge and solid, like dirty snowballs. They **orbit** far out into the solar system, much further than Pluto orbits. The first spacecraft to explore a comet was called *Giotto*. It was built in Britain and launched in 1985. The craft had a dust shield to protect it.

Giotto flew through Halley's Comet in March 1985.

analyse   examine something in detail
module   part of a spacecraft. It can exist by itself.

An artist's impression of *Galileo* orbiting Jupiter.

Halley's Comet comes close to the Earth every 76 years.

ASTEROIDS

Asteroids are rocky and look like the Moon. They are irregular in shape like potatoes. They orbit the Sun mainly between Mars and Jupiter.

Galileo took the first photographs of an asteroid called Gaspra, on its way to Jupiter. One spacecraft, called *Near*, orbited the asteroid Eros. It landed on its surface.

STARDUST

A mission, called Stardust, should bring dust back from comets and stars to Earth in 2006 for **analysis**. The largest asteroids, Ceres and Vesta, will be explored in 2010–14. The *Rosetta* craft will land a small **module** on to the centre of a comet.

SHOOTING AT COMETS

Deep Impact was launched in 2004. It will shoot a copper 'bullet' into the surface of comet P/Tempel 1. This will find out what the comet is made of.

BASE IN SPACE

Space stations provide a more permanent base in space. Scientists can carry out experiments, and observe space and Earth from them. Some people thought the first space station would be like a giant bicycle wheel. In fact it was a single **module**.

GOOD COMPANY!
The *Salyut 7* cosmonauts Anatoli Berezevoi and Valentini Lebedev argued right at the start of their 211-day mission. They spent the rest of the flight not talking to one another!

Salyut 7 space station seen from a Soyuz spacecraft.

>>>>>>>>>>
Find out more about Soyuz on pages 53 and 55.

depressurize   have a sudden loss of air from a cabin. A crew would die of suffocation if this happened.

RUSSIAN SALYUT

Salyut 1 was launched in 1971 and was 14.5 metres (47 feet) long. Soviet **cosmonauts** lived on board for three weeks. They were all tragically killed when their Soyuz spacecraft **depressurized** during **re-entry**.

In this picture the **astronaut** and scientist Owen Garriott is working aboard the US *Skylab* space station in 1973, during a 28-day mission.

US SKYLAB

The USA launched a space station called *Skylab* in 1973. This was an upper stage of a Saturn **rocket**. It was converted into a hi-tech laboratory and had a **telescope** attached to it.

Three **crews** were aboard the lab until 1974. Each crew had three people. One crew, Gerry Carr, Ed Gibson and Bill Pogue, made a record-breaking 84-day mission. *Skylab* was abandoned in 1974 and re-entered the Earth's **atmosphere** in 1979. Most of it fell in the sea, but some bits fell on Australia.

America's first space station, *Skylab*, seen in **orbit** in 1973.

MISSION TO MARS

Information from long missions will help prepare people to go to Mars. The round journey to Mars will take two years.

TECH TALK

Skylab was 36 metres (118 feet) long and had a **mass** of 90 tonnes. It was made up of an Apollo ferry craft, **docking** adapter, solar observatory, airlock module and workshop. Its **solar arrays** had a span of 27 metres (88 feet).

---

solar arrays   wing-like structures that contain thousands of solar cells. Solar cells convert sunlight into electricity.

THE CHINESE JOIN IN

China is planning a space station. The first Chinese person has already been in space. Yang Liwei made a 21-hour flight in 2003. A Shenzhou spacecraft (right) will eventually dock to a **crewed** space station.

MIR

Imagine floating around in a space station for over 437 days. That is what a Soviet **cosmonaut** and doctor, Valeri Poliakov, did aboard the *Mir* space station. Sergei Avdeyev spent nearly two years in space during three shifts aboard *Mir*.

The *Mir* space station had a **mass** of about 100 tonnes and had five main **modules**. Each one was about the size of a single decker bus. A single **docking** unit with several ports connected these together. The first module was launched in 1986. In 1999 *Mir* was allowed to re-enter the Earth's **atmosphere** and burn up.

TECH TALK

Mir missions have taught us a lot about the effects of long spaceflights. The main effect is weak muscles, especially the heart. It is very important for people to exercise properly.

cosmonaut   space traveller from the former Soviet Union
dock   join up with another spacecraft in space

HIGH MAINTENANCE

Mir was a great success. Crews were aboard it permanently for ten years. Many parts did break down or had to be repaired. *Mir* was often criticized for this. This was unfair. A space station or any other vehicle will always need a certain amount of maintenance to operate for long periods.

Cosmonaut Yuri Romanenko is seen here aboard the *Mir* space station.

The *Mir* space station in **orbit**. It is seen from the Space Shuttle during a joint US–Russian mission.

OTHER MIR PIONEERS

Yuri Romanenko made a 326-day flight on *Mir* in 1987. Sergei Krikalev was on *Mir* for 311 days. He was also the first Russian to fly on the *International Space Station (ISS)*.

> > > > > > > > > > >

Find out more about the *International Space Station* on pages 51–53 and 55.

module   part of a spacecraft. It can exist by itself.

FREEDOM

NASA wanted to launch a large space station in the 1970s. At last, NASA's dream came true when the *Freedom* space station was given the go ahead, in 1984. It was supposed to have been finished in 1994 and was to have cost US $8 **billion**.

RUSSIA AND USA JOIN FORCES

The cost of *Freedom* grew as the first launch was delayed. NASA was about to cancel the project. Then Russia joined the *Freedom* project. It was renamed the *International Space Station* (*ISS*). Finally, in 1998, the first section was launched. The project had already cost US $90 billion.

ISS EQUIPMENT

The *ISS* has two Canadian-built **robot** arm systems and a mobile transporter. The transporter will travel along tracks outside the *ISS* and carry tools for **spacewalking** crew.

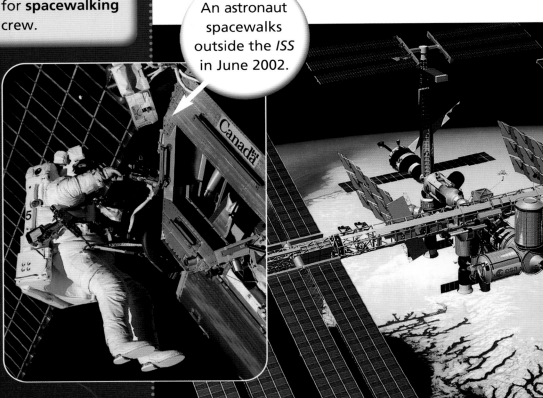

An astronaut spacewalks outside the *ISS* in June 2002.

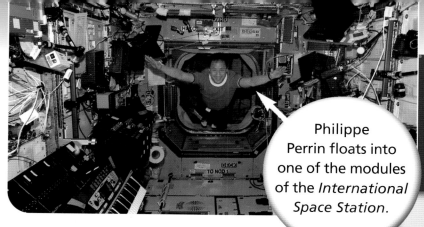

Philippe Perrin floats into one of the modules of the *International Space Station*.

BUILDING THE ISS

When the *ISS* is completed in about 2007, it will be the same size as a football pitch. It will provide the same working space as a Jumbo jet.

To finish the space station there will have to be over 45 Shuttle missions. Russia transports much of the **crew** and **cargo**, using their Progress and Soyuz craft. There will be **modules** from the USA, Russia, Europe and Japan attached to the *ISS*.

The *International Space Station* will look like this when it is finished.

WIRED UP

In the *ISS*, the electrical power system is connected with nearly 13 kilometres (8 miles) of wire. There are 52 computers to operate the *ISS*.

TECH TALK

Four pairs of **solar arrays**, each 34 metres (112 feet) long and 11 metres (36 feet) wide, will each supply 23 kilowatts of electricity.

◄◄◄◄◄◄◄◄◄◄◄◄◄◄◄◄◄
Find out more about robot arm systems on page 30.

robot   machine that can carry out tasks without the help of people

THE FUTURE

The first 'guest' on a spacecraft was Vladimir Remek, from the former Czechoslovakia, in 1978. He flew in a Soviet spacecraft.

WORKING IN SPACE

Charlie Walker (right) was the first person employed to work in space. He was an **engineer** for McDonnell Douglas and developed a space experiment. He flew in the Space Shuttle in 1984 and ended up making 3 missions in 15 months – more than some NASA **astronauts**!

A US Senator, Jake Garn, flew on a US Space Shuttle mission as a 'guest' in 1985. This was to thank him for helping to approve **NASA**'s **budget**!

The first space tourist, Dennis Tito (far right). He is pictured with his two-man Russian crew.

◀◀◀◀◀◀◀◀◀◀◀◀◀◀◀
Find out more about weightlessness on page 24.

HOLIDAY ON SOYUZ

The first paying space tourist was an American called Dennis Tito. He flew aboard a Russian Soyuz TM spacecraft and spent a few days aboard the *International Space Station* in 2001. Tito paid US $12 million. Tourists are lined up for Soyuz flights. The cost of the fare will become lower, if there are more missions.

PASSENGER FLIGHTS

Short **suborbital** flights could be a popular form of space tourism. These would last fifteen minutes, with five minutes to experience the weightlessness of space. Passengers would pay thousands of dollars for a ride, rather than millions.

SUPERSONIC FLIGHT

A carrier plane took *Spaceship One* (*SS1*) up to 15 kilometres (9 miles). *SS1* was then released and fired its rocket. It reached an **altitude** of 21 kilometres (13 miles) and a top speed of 1490 kilometres (925 miles) per hour. This is faster than the **speed of sound**.

Spaceship One is the first rocket plane to be developed and piloted by a private company, Scaled Composites.

speed of sound   speed at which sound waves travel
suborbital   flight into space that does not go fast enough to go into orbit

55

EXPLORING SPACE FURTHER

For almost 50 years we have explored and used space. We have seen fantastic developments in a very short time. The first phase of space exploration is coming to an end.

The challenges we face now need even more amazing spacecraft. It will take much longer to develop these. The next 10 years of space exploration may well be less exciting than the first 50 years. However, since the US **rovers** *Spirit* and *Opportunity* landed on Mars in January 2004, there is new enthusiasm about exploring space.

ALL SET TO GO TO MARS

The USA plans to build a base on the Moon by 2020. They will explore the more distant planets from there. The Russians intend to send people to Mars by 2014.

This is Buzz Aldrin's footprint in the moon-dust.

This spacecraft should land on the Saturn moon, Titan, in late 2005. It will be released from *Cassini*.

light year   distance it takes light to travel for one year. This is nearly 6000 million kilometres each year.

FUTURE SPACECRAFT

How we use space is now big business. We will develop new and improved **satellites**, particularly for communications. We can improve **rockets** more, but to help spacecraft travel though space faster, we have to explore new **technology**.

Mars will be the main target in the future. There are plans to send more **landers** and rovers to Mars every two years to bring back samples to the Earth. Pluto, the only planet we have not explored, may get a visit in 2016. Scientists are developing new space **telescopes**. These will let us look further into the **universe**.

The most important task is to make space exploration cheaper. It will then be possible for more missions to go ahead.

TECH TALK

Light years
Light travels at a speed of 186 kilometres (116 miles) per second. At that speed it takes 8 years for the light from Sirius to reach Earth. The distance between them is called 8 **light years**.

UNIMAGINABLE!

It might take 9 months to fly to Mars, but flying to the brightest star in our sky, Sirius, would take over 350,000 years.

This is a picture of the universe 12 **billion** light years away from Earth.

orbiter   part of a spacecraft that goes into orbit
universe   everything that exists

SPACECRAFT FACTS

A SUMMARY OF THE VOSTOK ACHIEVEMENTS

Date	Spacecraft	Cosmonauts	Achievement
April 1961	Vostok1	Yuri Gagarin	First man in space
August 1961	Vostok 2	Gherman Titov	Flew for a day
11 August 1962 12 August 1962	Vostok 3 Vostok 4	Andrian Nikolyev Pavel Popovich	First two crewed spacecraft in orbit at the same time
June 1963	Vostok 5	Valeri Bykovsky	Five-day solo flight– longest solo human spaceflight in history
June 1963	Vostok 6	Valentina Tereshkova	First woman in space

EARLY SPACECRAFT

Spacecraft	Dates in operation	Number of craft launched	Nationality
Sputnik	1957–1958	3	USSR
Explorer	1958–2000	78	USA
Mercury	1959–1961	16 (6 crewed)	USA
Luna	1959–1976	24	USSR
Vostok	1961–1963	6	USSR
Ranger	1961–1965	9	USA
Gemini	1964–1966	13 (10 crewed)	USA

In total, 105 spacecraft have attempted to go to the Moon (**fly-by, orbit** or landing). Only 46 missions were successful.

The Space Shuttle has a **mass** of 2040 tonnes. This is about the same mass as 340 adult male African elephants.

fly-by   when a spacecraft flies past a planet, rather than orbiting it. The spacecraft has only one chance to observe.

Pioneer 10, Pioneer 11, Voyager 1 and Voyager 2 are all in deep space. Voyager 1 and 2 are still sending data back to Earth. Voyager 1 is the most distant human-made object from the Earth in space. These spacecraft are powered by nuclear energy.

The Apollo programme cost over US $20 billion. The launch mass of the Command Service Module was over 28,000 kilograms. Its base had a diameter of 3.9 metres (13 feet) and was 11 metres (36 feet) long.

MARS SPACECRAFT

Spacecraft (launch mass)	Landers	Launch date	Arrival date
Mars Global Surveyor (767 kilograms)	none	November 1996	September 1997
Mars Pathfinder (895 kilograms)	Sojourner	December 1996	July 1997
2001 Odyssey (758 kilograms)	none	April 2001	October 2001
Mars Express (1042 kilograms)	Beagle 2	June 2003	December 2004
Mars Explorer (1063 kilograms)	Spirit Opportunity	June 2003 July 2003	January 2004

nuclear energy   energy released when the nucleus of an atom changes. This is called a nuclear reaction.

FIND OUT MORE

BOOKS

Becklake, Sue, *See and Explore: Space, Stars, Planets and Spacecraft*
(Dorling Kindersley Publishing, 2003)

Farndon, John, *How Science Works: Rockets and Other Spacecraft*
(Franklin Watts, 2003)

Jefferis, David, *Monster Machines: Spacecraft*
(Raintree Steck-Vaughn, 2003)

WORLD WIDE WEB

If you want to find out more about spacecraft you can search the Internet using keywords like these:

Apollo	Challenger
deep space	Luna
Mars Explorer	Moon
planets	**rockets**
satellites	Space Shuttle
solar system	Vostok

Make your own keywords using headings or words from this book. The search tips opposite will help you to find the most useful websites.

ORGANIZATIONS

Keo programme
This time capsule will travel for 50,000 years. When it returns to Earth it will share our history with future humans. You can add a message of your own here.
www.keo.org

NASA
The official **NASA** website.
www.nasa.gov

Spaceflight now
Latest news on launches of all space missions around the world.
www.spaceflight now.com

World almanac for kids: Space craft
Facts and figures about spacecraft.
www.worldalmanac forkids.com

SEARCH TIPS

There are billions of pages on the Internet so it can be difficult to find exactly what you are looking for. If you just type in 'spacecraft' on a search engine like Google, you will get a list of 58 million web pages. These search skills will help you find useful websites more quickly.

- Use simple keywords, not whole sentences.
- Use two to six keywords in a search.
- Be precise – only use names of people, places or things.
- If you want to find words that go together, put quote marks around them, for example 'International Space Station'.
- Use the advanced section of your search engine.
- Use the + sign between keywords to find pages with all these words.

WHERE TO SEARCH

SEARCH ENGINE

A search engine looks through the entire web and lists all sites that match the search words. The best matches are at the top of the list, on the first page. Try bbc.co.uk/search

SEARCH DIRECTORY

A search directory is like a library of websites. You can search by keyword or subject and browse through the different sites like you look through books on a library shelf. A good example is yahooligans.com

GLOSSARY

altitude height of something above sea level

amplify make a signal stronger

analyse examine something in detail

ascent journey up

astronaut space traveller

astronomer person who studies stars and planets

atmosphere gases, liquids and solids that surround a planet

atmospheric pressure force of the atmosphere pressing down

billion number equal to one thousand million

broadcast give out information on the radio or television

budget amount of money put aside for a project

capsule part of a spacecraft, which comes apart from the rest

cargo things that are carried on a vehicle, such as a satellite on a Space Shuttle

clamp something that holds two parts together very tightly

cockpit area where the pilot controls the spacecraft

commercial organizations that make money

cosmonaut space traveller from the former Soviet Union

crater large hollow, shaped like a bowl

crew people that operate the spacecraft

data information or scientific measurements

depressurize sudden loss of air from a cabin. A crew would die of suffocation if this happened.

descent journey down

diameter distance from one side of a circle to another through the centre

dock join up with another spacecraft in space

engineer person who uses science to design, build, control and use machines

environment conditions around you

erect build so that it is upright

EVA Extra-Vehicular Activity, or activity outside the vehicle

exhaust waste gases from an engine

external outside

fly-by when a spacecraft flies past a planet, rather than orbiting it. The spacecraft has only one chance to observe.

friction when one object rubs against another. This causes heat.

fuselage body of the spacecraft

galaxy group of stars in space

gravity force of a large body, like Earth, on smaller objects

lander part of the spacecraft that lands on the planet to be explored

light year distance it takes light to travel for one year. This is nearly 6000 million kilometres each year.

lunar about the Moon

mass how much there is of something

microbe tiny living thing that can be seen under a microscope

micrometeoroid particle of dust in space that travels very fast

missile rocket with a warhead

module part of a spacecraft. It can exist by itself.

monitor watch over something regularly

NASA National Aeronautics and Space Agency

navigation method of finding the position of something or the correct route

nuclear energy energy released when the nucleus of an atom changes. This is called a nuclear reaction

orbit curved path followed by something around a large object in space

orbiter part of a spacecraft that goes into orbit

payload bay area or space where most of the cargo is stored

plummet fall very quickly

pollution harmful substances in the environment

radiation energy, such as light and heat, that can travel through space

reconnaissance looking closely at an area, especially by the military

re-entry high-speed return of a space vehicle through the Earth's atmosphere

rendezvous get close to another spacecraft in orbit

robot machine that can carry out tasks without the help of people

rocket machine that gives a spacecraft the speed it needs to reach space

rotate turn around an axis or central point

rover space vehicle with wheels

satellite object that goes around a much larger body, like Earth, in space

solar arrays wing-like structures that contain thousands of solar cells. Solar cells convert sunlight into electricity.

solar system Sun and the planets that move around it

spacewalk move about outside the spacecraft in space

speed of sound speed at which sound waves travel

sphere circular solid that is shaped like a ball

suborbital flight into space that does not go fast enough to go into orbit

sulphur yellow, non-metal, chemical element

super power country with immense political and military influence throughout the world

technology use of science

telescope instrument that uses mirrors and lenses to view distant objects

tether wire that attaches an astronaut to the spacecraft

thrust force produced by engine to propel a spacecraft through space

turbulent fast moving in all directions

universe everything that exists

ventilator machine that gets air to flow into a small space, like a spacesuit

zero-gravity when there is no gravity

INDEX

Titles in the *Mean Machines* series include:

BOATS

Hardback   1 844 43164 9

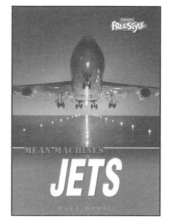

JETS

Hardback   1 844 43161 4

MILITARY AIRCRAFT

Hardback   1 844 43172 X

MONSTER TRUCKS

Hardback   1 844 43174 6

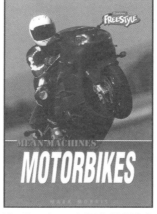

MOTORBIKES

Hardback   1 844 43163 0

RACING CARS

Hardback   1 844 43162 2

SPACECRAFT

Hardback   1 844 43173 8

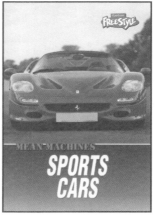

SPORTS CARS

Hardback   1 844 43171 1

Find out about the other titles in this series on our website www.raintreepublishers.co.uk

THE SPIRIT OF

GLASGOW

THE SPIRIT OF
GLASGOW

ROBIN WARD

RICHARD DREW PUBLISHING · GLASGOW

For Porta

Half title: *Glasgow Coat of Arms on a tramcar in the Transport Museum.*
Title page: *The 19th-century Connal Building reflected in the modern
façade of the Clydesdale Bank, West George Street.*

Great Western Road, Glasgow in 1924

Richard Drew Publishing Limited
6 Clairmont Gardens
Glasgow G3 7LW
Scotland

First published 1984
© Robin Ward
ISBN 0 86267 057 8

Designed by Robin Ward
Photoset in Perpetua by Face Ronchetti Limited, London
Colour separations by CMR Graphics, East Kilbride
Printed and bound by William Collins Sons & Company Limited, Glasgow

When Ferdinand de Lesseps got bogged down in Egypt while digging the Suez Canal he didn't think twice about where to find help. He hired some Scottish engineers from Glasgow.

Glasgow? Yes, Glasgow. From the mid-19th until well into the 20th century Scotland's largest city was pre-eminent in the fields of mechanical and marine engineering, shipbuilding and other heavy industries. It was a self-made city state whose engineers had blasted their way up the shallow, meandering River Clyde, creating a waterway for ocean-going ships to reach the city centre, capturing for Glasgow an import-export trade which the railways might otherwise have taken to Leith, Liverpool or London.

Glasgow was *the* Victorian city, a sprawling, sulphureous metropolis of iron foundries, locomotive works, shipyards and steelworks – and squalid, overcrowded slums. It also had its share of elegant parks and boulevards, and above all, it had its architecture. This was the medium in which Glasgow's industrial and mercantile moguls chose to express and represent themselves – and how they built. Glasgow is a mighty city of noble commercial and civic façades, relics of the time when it was the workshop and the second city of the greatest empire the world has known.

Today, Glasgow's status has shrunk, its prosperity and trade patterns being too closely linked to a vanished empire. It is a city only now, belatedly, coming to terms with its swift decline. In the 1960s the city's official response to this decline seemed to involve the obliteration of all traces of the Victorian city in a hectic, perverse effort to modernise. This process stumbled to a halt, wounded by volleys of criticism and a growing awareness that Glasgow's incomparable 19th-century buildings were irreplaceable symbols of the city's spirit and past splendour.

Stone-cleaned and restored, Glasgow's Victorian buildings have now become symbols, not of decline, but of renaissance. They stand as reminders of the time when Glasgow was a great city and they give credence to its claim that it still is. They are reference points, buttresses against mediocre modernisation, demanding by comparison that the modern city being built around them should aspire to their spirit and quality.

Glasgow is still the commerical, industrial and artistic capital of Scotland – as it was at the turn of the century. It still has its share of urban problems, but it has these in common with just about every large conurbation in the world. Its reputation for urban violence and deprivation, while not wholly false, is exaggerated. Behind the hostile, macho stare and the abrasive accent, the city which challenges the world with an aggressive 'See you, Jimmy', has a soft centre. People talk to you in Glasgow.

Glaswegians are friendly, funny and refreshingly outspoken. They are used to getting things done. Those who become successful tend to be as self-made as their city. People respect this and despite its almost Third World social inequalities, the city is not plagued by pretensions or social jealousies. Glaswegians are also stubborn and independent. This makes them, for example, suicidal jay-walkers. They jump out in front of cars, giving drivers the 'See you, Jimmy' look, daring to be run down. In Glasgow pedestrians may not officially have the right of way, but they certainly act as if they do. In this respect they are no different from their forefathers who pioneered trade routes across the globe. They never doubted their right of way, whether they were building railways across Canada, running steamers on the rivers of Burma or trading in Hong Kong.

Glasgow's people are intensely proud of their feisty city, and are quick to tell you of its history and merits. They may be Scottish, but will always be Glaswegians first. Their ethnic culture is outward-looking rather than provincial. Arriving in Glasgow from London, or even Edinburgh, is like entering an unknown foreign metropolis. The local accent is not exactly English, and visually, Glasgow has the look more of a great European or American 19th-century city rather than of a British one. Its unique history and irrepressible people have made it so, and I hope this book reflects and illustrates its spirit and character.

Robin Ward, February 1984

Victorian Glasgow preserved:
The view from Ruchill Park showing the late
19th-century tenements of North Woodside, the
Kibble Palace (1873) in Botanic Gardens,
Kelvinside Free Church (1862), Grosvenor
Terrace (1855) in Great Western Road,
Dowanhill Church (1865) and, beyond, the cranes
of Govan Shipbuilders.

The Parisian roofline of Glasgow's Park Terrace (1855) seen from Kelvingrove Park:
The park was designed by Charles Wilson and opened in 1855. It was described at the time as 'a delightful retreat ... unrivalled as a place for quiet and meditative enjoyment', which it still is today. Park Terrace and its environs, also designed by Charles Wilson and built on the top of Woodlands Hill, rank with the best in Europe as an example of visionary 19th-century town planning.

The last twenty years have seen Glasgow's skyline littered with anonymous high-rise towers and familiar city streets replaced by a weave of expressways. Vast areas of the city were cleared of 'slum' tenements, bulldozed in a grand plan to transform the great, grimy Victorian metropolis into 'the most modern city in Europe'. The trouble was that Glaswegians had a soft spot for their old city. They liked their 19th-century tenements and tramway system. The convenience of driving from one end of the city to another in ten minutes was an irrelevance to non-car owners and once the novelty of waving to aeroplanes wore off they found high-rise living pretty unpleasant.

The planners don't build tower blocks and motorways any more. Their dream of turning Glasgow into a film set to remake Fritz Lang's *Metropolis* went over budget and the money to fulfil it has run out. The days when the city's mandarins behaved like Cecil B de Mille and the architects used people as bit players and extras on their models have passed. Enough remains of the city's 19th-century architectural glory for it to be appreciated today and, it has to be said, it gains in stature by being juxtaposed with the half-built modern city which was to have replaced it.

left: *'The most modern city in Europe.' The half-built vision of the 1960s.*
above: *The Victorian city, showing (left to right) St Mary's Cathedral (1893), Woodlands UF Church (1876), the Florentine towers of Free Church College (1861) and Park Church (1858).*

Glasgow's city centre escaped the scourge of comprehensive redevelopment which sent many inner-city suburbs to oblivion. It remains much as originally built in the 19th century, densely packed with a rich incomparable heritage of Victorian commercial architecture. Two buildings which symbolise the spirit of that time more than any others are the City Chambers and the Central Station Hotel.

Glasgow's City Chambers was inaugurated in 1888 by no less than Queen Victoria herself, an event witnessed by a huge crowd of citizens in George Square. The city fathers wanted a building to reflect Glasgow's position as the 'Second City of the Empire.' They certainly got one. It is a Victorian town hall to eclipse all others and its opulence reflects the city's civic and imperial pomp and pride.

It was designed in Baroque/Renaissance style by William Young, a London Scot who hailed from Paisley. The building is as decorative as the famous textile patterns that came from that town. While the façade projects a feeling of rather pompous Scottish integrity, inside the design is wonderfully over-the-top. It feels like the Palace of Versailles. There are grand stairways of Italian Carrara marble rising three floors, Venetian glass windows and mosaics, Aberdeen granite stonework, Spanish mahogany fittings, ornamental coloured ceramic work and a lobby designed to look like a church of the Italian Renaissance. The building abounds with statues and painted panels declaring Victorian virtues; Wisdom, Purity, Strength, Honour, Justice, Modesty (which seems out of place in such an interior), Faith, Hope, and Charity, all designed to elevate and enlighten.

left: *The floodlit tower and (right) the entrance hall of the City Chambers.*
far right: *The clock tower and floodlit façade of the Central Hotel.*

The architect hoped that his building would be '…one of the most lasting monuments which they (Glasgow's citizens) will leave to tell to future generations of the marvellously rapid growth and energy of the city…' He wasn't far wrong.

Glasgow Central Station and its hotel were also built for prestige as well as practical purposes. The Victorian railway companies, like the municipal authorities, had architecturally exalted views of their own importance. They built monolithic railway stations and hotels across Europe and America with façades designed to look like Florentine palazzos, Greek temples and Gothic cathedrals – any style in fact that would lend an aura of respectability and power to their works. The Central Hotel (1884), built by the Caledonian Railway Company, is no exception. It is more graceful than most and its Scottish/Scandinavian Renaissance style seems more appropriate to its northern location than, say, a building which looked like the Parthenon would have been. Its massive clock tower can be seen from miles away.

The City Chambers and the Central Hotel crown a rich layer of 19th-century architecture which covers the American-style grid plan of Glasgow's city centre. The city's Victorian architects managed to produce buildings and streetscapes of astonishing variety and distinction. They were sponsored by wealthy industrialists, merchants and bankers who wished to outshine their rivals and collectively boost the city's growing imperial stature. At every turn a new exciting vista opens up or an ornate façade is glimpsed a block away through a narrow lane. Some streets plumb canyon-like depths between tall Victorian office blocks. Others take a rollercoaster ride up and down the city's hilly townscape.

The city centre grid plan, imposed almost fanatically on the series of *drumlins* (volcanic ridges) on which Glasgow is built, not only makes it one of the hilliest cities in Europe, but has created spectacular townscape effects – combinations of space, sky and perspectives – which make it such an exciting place to explore.

Glasgow's visual appearance owes little to other British cities. Glasgow's architects

rarely worked elsewhere and consequently remain little known outside the city. They drew their influences direct from Europe and America, rather than via London, and bypassed contemporary English fashion. Glasgow feels more like a great European city than a British one.

Most Victorian architects could do little more than imitate the glories of ancient Greece and Rome. Some, especially in Glasgow, were more original. Alexander 'Greek' Thomson, for example, was designing adventurous Graeco/Egyptian churches in Glasgow in a highly personal style while contemporaries were copying picture books of Athens. 'Greek' Thomson was also influenced by the 19th-century German architect Schinkel, which is why parts of the city look like pre-war Berlin. Indeed, Glasgow's special architectural character is its mixture of traditional Scottish styles and references from many other countries. Charing Cross Mansions could be in Paris. The style of Templeton's Carpet Factory is Venetian. The 19th-century cast-iron warehouses could be in New York, the massive 1920s office blocks in Chicago and the Art Galleries in *fin-de-siècle* Vienna. Above the shopfronts, Glasgow abounds with similar and often more bizarre cross-cultural connections which enhance the city's splendid architectural heritage.

far left: *The German Renaissance-style Connal Building (1900) in West George Street. With typical Victorian ostentation the owner illustrated his business interests on the façade. There are steam locomotives, Clyde-built ships and carved images of local inventors and industrialists, among them James Watt (father of the steam engine), James Neilson (inventor of the hot blast furnace) and, not to be outdone, the owner himself, William Connal, one of the city's business barons.*
left: *'Canyon-like depths', Mitchell Lane looking towards Buchanan Street.*
right: *'Façades glimpsed from a block away.' The Clydesdale Bank (1896) in Buchanan Street, once one of the renowned Cranston tearooms.*

right: *St George's Tron Church (1807) framed by the cupolas and cornices of Victorian commerce.*
above: *1920s art deco and 1850s Glasgow Venetian Renaissance details in West Nile Street.*
below: *Two Titans supporting the former St Andrew's Halls (1877) seem to symbolise the burden of preserving historic buildings in a changing world. In this case, they represent some hope, as the frontage of the fire-gutted halls was recently restored and incorporated into the adjacent Mitchell Library.*

above: *The intricate, lacey detail on the cast-iron façade of the Ca d'Oro building (1872) in Gordon Street.*
below: *Façade detail on 'Greek' Thomson's Egyptian Halls (1873) in Union Street. The row of chubby columns propping up the cornice ought to be on the banks of the Nile rather than close to the Clyde.*

'A city of spectacular topographic effects':
left: *Looking west up St Vincent Street. The Egyptianesque tower of 'Greek' Thomson's St Vincent Street Church dominates the skyline.*
above: *Looking up Renfield Street.*
below: *Above West George Street, winter sunlight paints the Victorian city with a warm glow.*
right: *Hope Street looking north showing the monumental scale of the Central Hotel clock tower.*

The apparently precipitous plunge down Hope Street seen from Cowcaddens. On the left in the middle distance is Lion Chambers. Further down and half-hidden by the drop is the cupola of the flamboyantly designed and evocatively named Liverpool, London and Globe Insurance Building, and, visible as always, the gabled tower of the Central Hotel.

Despite fairly widespread demolition many Glasgow street scenes seem little changed since the late Victorian/Edwardian period. St Andrew's Cross Mansions (left) at Eglinton Toll remain and have been recently renovated. However, the power station chimneys belching smoke towards the East End, giving the 19th-century merchants and bankers a good reason to move west where they could escape the fumes carried by the prevailing wind, have been swept away.

The trams (below left) have disappeared from Jamaica Bridge along with its ornamental cast-iron lamp standards, but the photographer (Annan) would still recognise the view today. He'd be a bit bamboozled though by Charing Cross (top right). The Grand Hotel has vanished, demolished in the late 1960s to make way for a huge trench in the ground which carries the Ring Road around the city's west flank. The rippling curved façade of Charing Cross Mansions (1891), designed by Sir J J Burnet, was fortunately spared. It still stands today, the ultimate elaboration of Glasgow tenement design.

Further east along Sauchiehall Street (right) very few of the buildings in this 1905 view survive. The famous department stores, Copland's and Pettigrew's on the right, are now only a memory. Yet the street and the other locations on this page are still vividly recognisable due to the Victorian landmarks which remain. This architectural continuity is important for all cities, providing an identity and historical touchstone which transcends generations in a way more recent development has yet to achieve.

SITTINGROOM WINDOW ON GARDNER ST PARTICK
No 42 CAIRD DRIVE
GLASGOW W1

24

Glasgow's most characteristic buildings are its tenements. Until recently, they were seen as dilapidated symbols of a past era, and their destruction as a sign of 'progress'. Whole communities of 19th-century city tenements were enthusiastically obliterated in the comprehensive redevelopment of the 1960s. But today, the rot has stopped. Tenements are back in fashion. Enterprising housing associations backed by government and local authority grants have given the city's surviving tenement areas a new lease of life. Buildings which were black with industrial grime have been stone-cleaned, revealing the beautiful honey-coloured and red sandstone with which they were originally built. Interiors have been renovated to become desirable homes once again and, as a result, a large part of Glasgow's domestic architectural heritage has been saved.

Scotland has a long tradition of tenement building and this reached its height of expression in 19th-century Glasgow. The city's tenement architects and builders designed incredibly long tenement rows which stride up and down the city's hilly topography with panache and virtuosity, creating some stunning urban vistas. Most were built in the industrial Klondike years 1870-1910 to house a rapidly growing population. Contrary to popular belief and their 'slum' reputation, many were designed for Glasgow's prosperous bourgeoisie as well as for factory workers. The preserved Tenement House in Buccleuch Street, run by the National Trust for Scotland, is a good example of one of these better quality city tenements.

Glasgow's tenements achieve a robust architectural dignity rarely found in the mass-housing of other 19th-century cities. Most of their façades copy the architectural proportions of, believe it or not, Italian Renaissance palazzos. Social pretensions were flattered in a variety of other architectural styles – Greek, Egyptian, French Second Empire and Gothic. Many tenements display the Victorians' delight in superfluous but charming decoration with

stained or painted glass windows, colourfully glazed floral tiles and occasional sculpture.

The city tenement areas fostered a strong sense of community. The design of these buildings helped this communal lifestyle develop – the shared entrance close and stairway where children could gather on rainy days, the backcourt where mothers could hang the laundry and keep an eye on the *weans* playing, and the proximity of other tenements across the street where conversations could take place hanging out of your second storey window. They are also amongst the friendliest areas in the city.

The sense of place which these areas bred was so strong that when many people were decamped to housing schemes on the city boundary during redevelopment they kept returning to their wrecked communities. This explains the peculiar Glasgow sight of urban wastelands on which the only surviving buildings are the local bars. No people live here but the bars survive, their customers travelling from across the city to visit their old haunts. Many of Glasgow's tenements were indeed slums. Overcrowding and squalor seemed to require the sweeping solution of wholesale destruction. But in the process many healthy communities were destroyed. Today, belated and moderately successful attempts are being made to rebuild them while preserving those which remain.

'Striding up and down the city's hilly topography with panache and virtuosity, creating stunning urban vistas.'
above and far left: *Tenementscape in Gardner Street, Partick.*
left: *Honey-coloured sandstone, Gardner Street.*

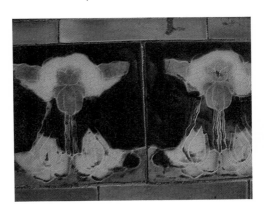

above and opposite page: *Painted glass tenement stairway window.*

left: *Art nouveau and other floral 'wally close' tiles.*

below: *Cast-iron hearth in the preserved Tenement House.*

above and below: *Breadalbane Terrace (1845) on Hill Street, before and after renovation.*

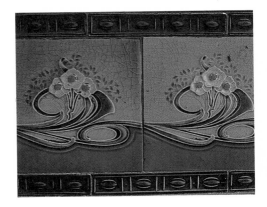

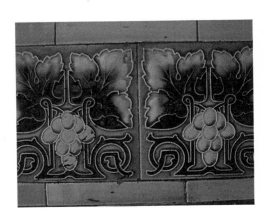

28

Tenement life as it was...
opposite page: *Braeside Street, Maryhill, with chimney sweeps crossing the road. In the background, the Park Towers.*
left: *Street children in Springburn.*
right: *Backcourt canyon, Springburn.*

left: *Children in a closemouth, Willowbank Street, Woodlands.*
right: *The old and the new, Woodside.*
opposite page: *Dilapidated streetscape at St George's Cross, once a major shopping area and tramway junction; the buildings shown on the right and left still stand, awaiting renovation.*

30

If Glasgow's tenement areas have been transformed, whether through demolition or restoration, this is nothing compared to what has happened to the River Clyde. In the late 19th and early 20th centuries this was the foremost waterway of the world. Between 1870 and 1914 the Clyde shipyards alone built 18 per cent of the world's steamships. At their peak just before the First World War this was approaching one-third. Today, only footprints remain of this proud industry. The river which saw the launching of the *Cutty Sark*, the Cunard 'Queens' and *HMS Hood* now flows silently to the sea. The forest of cranes lining its banks has largely disappeared. The shipping lines which offered passages to Cairo, Bombay and Brisbane, New York, Vancouver or Valparaiso have vanished almost without trace. So too the Clyde-built coastal paddle steamers and little ferries which skittishly plied the river. Only the *Waverley*, the 'last sea-going paddle steamer in the world' continues the Glasgow holiday tradition of sailing 'doon the watter'.

this page:
top left: *Govan Shipbuilders seen from the stern of the 'Waverley' on a summer morning.*
centre: *Sailing 'doon the watter' to the melodies of an accordianist.*
right: *The final moments at Queen's Dock. Now completely filled in, the dock is the site for the new Scottish Exhibition Centre.*
above: *A faded sign at Meadowside Quay advertising long abandoned passenger sailings to Australia.*

opposite page:
top left: *The Finnieston Crane, a surviving monolith designed to load boilers and steam locomotives on board cargo ships. It may yet become a tourist attraction.*
centre: *Queen's Dock, opened in 1880, showing a forlorn sign one hundred years later.*
right: *The PS 'Waverley', built in Glasgow in 1947, cruising the Firth of Clyde.*

opposte page: *The Govan Ferry crossing the Clyde. This service, the last of its kind, was recently withdrawn. Beyond are the cranes of Govan and Meadowside Granary.*

The Clyde as it was...
top left: *Buzzing like busy bees , the Clyde steamers 'Daniel Adamson', 'Iona' and 'Benmore' at Broomielaw in 1895.*
bottom left: *General Terminus Quay, where vast quantities of iron ore were unloaded for the steelworks of Lanarkshire.*
above: *The South Basin of Queen's Dock (c1890). Queen's Dock offered berthage for Glasgow shipping lines sailing to the Mediterrranean, South America, Burma and Australia.*

'Footprints of a proud industry':
The old Fairfield Shipyard, symbol of a
shipbuilding tradition going back over 150 years.
Many great ships were built here, the Empress
liners for the Canadian Pacific, battleships for the
Royal Navy and even a yacht for the Tsar of
Russia. Now Govan Shipbuilders, the yard
precariously survives, a phantom image of
Victorian industrial grandeur.

opposite page: *'We were really proud to build that wonderful ship.' The launching of the 'Queen Mary' at John Brown's Clydebank yard (1934). The yard today is more prosaic. It has changed owners several times and now builds oil rigs and production platforms for the North Sea.*

this page:

top left and right: *'We don't just build ships here, we build men.' Welders at Govan Shipbuilders.*

below: *The battle-cruiser 'HMS Hood', 'pride of the Royal Navy', leaving Clydebank in 1920.*

At the turn of the century the industrial products from Glasgow's iron foundries, shipyards and many engineering works dominated the imperial markets. Pre-eminent were the shipyards and the locomotive builders. While every important port in the world probably had a Clyde-built ship in the harbour at any given time, it was said that wherever there were railways, Glasgow-built locomotives were running on them.

In 1903, when the famed North British Locomotive Company was formed in Glasgow by the amalgamation of three pioneering firms, the new conglomerate became the largest producer of steam locomotives in Europe. Most of its production was exported and the list of countries to which its railway engines were supplied reads like the index of an atlas. The most important markets were India and South Africa (where NB steam engines still

run today), South America, Australia, New Zealand and Britain. Only Baldwins and the American Locomotive Company in the USA could boast greater capacity.

A memorable and almost daily sight in Glasgow at the time was to see one of these huge steam engines being hauled down Springburn Road by a team of Clydesdale horses or on a low-loader to the docks for export, visible evidence of the city's productivity and prosperity. Sadly, the

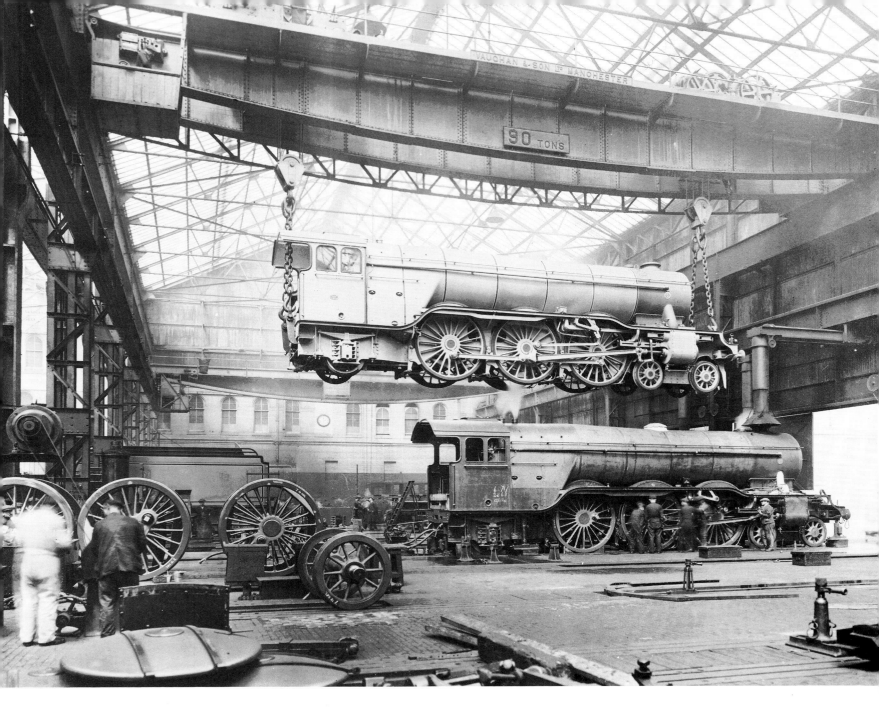

opposite page: *A North British locomotive destined for East African Railways about to be swung aboard a ship by the Finnieston Crane.*
above: *An evocative industrial scene in the Hydepark Locomotive Works, Springburn. Springburn in North Glasgow had the highest concentration of locomotive works in the city.*
left: *A locomotive being hauled down Springburn Road.*

North British is no more. It was liquidated in 1962, having belatedly and unsuccessfully attempted to change to diesel production.

In common with other Victorian cities, Glasgow had several main line railway stations and a spidery network of suburban and subway lines. The most important and impressive of the remaining main line stations is Glasgow Central, departure point for the Clyde Coast, England and the Continent. Queen Street Station nearby serves the Highland lines, Edinburgh and Aberdeen.

Once through the cast-iron gateway at Glasgow Central, travellers enter a sun-dappled, spacious Victorian concourse of polished woodwork, sandstone, and fanlight windows, spanned by a sprawling canopy of iron and glass. The railway lines in and out are all electrified, the signalling is computerised and the station is one of the busiest in Europe, yet it has managed to maintain its late 19th-century atmosphere.

One device which has escaped computerisation and helps preserve the authentic Victorian aura in the station is the

huge pre-1914 wooden train information booth, operated by an army of wee men who shuffle the large destination boards from window to window. There's no excuse for missing your train here with such an admirably legible information system.

this page:
above: *Detail of the cast-iron entrance canopy.*
above left: *'Fanlight windows spanned by a sprawling canopy of iron and glass.'*
left: *The glazed iron and glass arches of the 'Hielandman's Umbrella' (the bridge crossing Argyle Street) which was a sheltered meeting place for Glasgow's 19th-century Highland immigrants.*

opposite page:
top: *The huge pre-1914 train indicator display.*
bottom: *Passengers watching departure times.*
far left: *Parisian style canopy over the entrance to one of the Central Hotel's French restaurants.*

Glasgow's railway and shipbuilding history is commemorated in the Transport Museum, currently housed in a converted tramway depot in Albert Drive. Here you can find several Glasgow-built locomotives and, in the Clyde Room, an unrivalled collection of shipbuilder's models. However the most popular exhibits are probably the tramcars and a re-creation of a Glasgow District Subway station.

The Subway was first opened in 1896 as a cable-hauled system. It was electrified in 1935 and completely modernised in the late 1970s. When it was eventually closed for modernisation in 1977, some of the original cars were still in service. Two of these have found their way to the Transport Museum.

The old Subway was a popular friendly system. There's nothing wrong with the modern version either. It's just too new for Glaswegians to be sentimental about, although it already has a nickname, the 'Clockwork Orange', a reference to the new colour of the coaches and the fact that, compared to New York or Paris, it's more like a Hornby toy train set. It goes round and round in a circle and is impossible to get lost in. If you miss your stop, you just keep going until you come back round again about half an hour later. When the system was electrified in the 1930s the Corporation changed the name from Subway to Underground, mainly for the cachet of association with the much larger London system. True Glaswegians of course never liked this. They stubbornly stuck to calling it the Subway and probably always will.

Glaswegians do have a sentimental streak, a feeling for times past. After all, you can't escape the past in the city. It is all around. The ghosts of shipbuilders, engineers and locomotive manufacturers and the aristocracy of imperial commerce stare impassively down from the façades of the city's Victorian buildings. If anything is calculated to make Glaswegians dewy-eyed it is talk of the city's tramway system. Tramways, originally horse-drawn and electrified in 1901, ran on the city's streets from 1872 to 1962 when the system was

abandoned. With over 250 miles of track it was one of the most extensive and efficient in Europe. Unlike the buses which replaced them, the trams were 'reliable vehicles which rarely left the rails and almost always stopped at the stops'. They created their own folklore. Everyone had a favourite colour or route number or knew a friendly conductor who would take a 'personal interest in passengers' well-being and protect drunks from thieves'. And there was a tramway language, a version of the Glasgow patois. Conductors' cries of 'cumoangerraff' or 'seeyouse, ahmraoneyyin allood taeopenrawindae' could be heard as the 'caurs' rattled by.

When the system closed 250,000 people turned out to witness the Last Tram Procession. Many citizens still lament their passing. Even today city shops sell tramway ephemera – books, prints and other knick-knacks – in large quantities. It was said that the trams caused traffic congestion, but soon after they were replaced it was admitted in some quarters that the whole exercise had been 'a huge waste of time and money'. Perhaps now that the Ring Road has relieved the city centre of chaotic traffic jams the trams will soon return – a city centre service linking railway and bus stations and shopping areas would be feasible. Most Glaswegians would be happy to see it happen. Meanwhile they continue to take their children on sentimental journeys to Albert Drive.

far left: *Coronation tram No 1173 in Glasgow's Museum of Transport.*
above: *The Subway Gallery, a re-creation of Merkland Street station in the Transport Museum.*

'Where are the trams of yesteryear
The pride and joy of rich and poor
Upon their passing shed a tear
Ah! Auchenshuggle, oh! Dalmuir.'
(verse from the Glasgow Herald)
Left: *Tramcar destination rollers in the Transport Museum.*

In some aspects, Glasgow does seem to have become 'the most modern city in Europe'. It has a modern subway system which is complemented above ground by electric suburban railways and extensive bus routes. It has a large modern airport which (Glaswegians are fond of such extravagant claims) is at one end of the busiest airline route in Europe – from London. But it is only when driving on the city's Ring Road that the planners' dream really comes true. Here you could be on the freeways of Los Angeles, except that the exit signs say 'Clyde Tunnel', 'Provanmill Gas Works' or

'Easterhouse', which is a long way from Sunset Boulevard. And yet, at twilight, approaching the city from the airport under the tall string of motorway lights, as you curve up the ramp of the Kingston Bridge and glimpse the fluorescent blocks of modern commerce beyond, you do get the insinuating impression of entering a modern city. But it is not Glasgow. It may seem romantic in a jet-setting way, but the vision you see in the twilight could be Bangkok, New York, even, if you ignore the exit signs, Los Angeles.

left: *Glasgow's Ring Road crossing the Kingston Bridge.*
above: *Glasgow's concrete jungle under the approach ramps of the Kingston Bridge.*

Below the elevated motorways or bypassed by the expressways lie forgotten areas of the city – quiet, desolate backwaters, temporary creeks in the wake of redevelopment.

Mr Swift in Springburn lived up to his name helping people move when an expressway was bulldozed through their area. In fact, he's done his job so well that there's hardly anyone left now. His shop is closed and he'll be removing himself soon.

The Scottish Wholesale Co-operative Society buildings in Morrison Street are opulent enough to be in the city centre — but they stand in decaying grandeur, isolated from the rest of the city by the river and the motorway approaches to the Kingston Bridge. Once a bustling warehouse and waterfront area, Morrison Street manages to look beautiful in decline, reminiscent of the picturesque but melancholy Vienna of 'The Third Man'.

48

above: *The gritty Loweryesque beauty of Glasgow's post-industrial districts . . . small cash-only backstreet businesses which make the city seem like Naples, derelict factories, lonely tenement blocks, makeshift football pitches and desultory groups of people.*
left and below: *The new Gorbals.*

Picturesque is not how you would describe these tower blocks (left) in the Gorbals. This is the Glasgow that the tourists have all probably heard about but are seldom encouraged to see. You can see why. The architecture is brutal and ugly. Surely this is not the finest Victorian city in Europe.

These buildings replaced the violent tenement slums of *No Mean City*.

Architecturally the old Gorbals looked better than this and its reputation for Chicago-style gangsters was exaggerated. The only bonus that these tower blocks can offer is that where in a single-end (one room) tenement flat you could barely swing a cat, here on these featureless windy housing schemes there's plenty of space to play with the dog.

left: *Buskers in Argyle Street. A local bylaw now allows shoppers to be serenaded. Some of these musicians, like the band shown, are very good, some are so-so, others are simply dreadful.*
centre left: *The Argyll Arcade (1827). An early use of iron and glass construction, it is also the centre of Glasgow's jewellery trade.*
bottom left: *'Remember sweets for the children' . . . a mouth-watering display of confections likely to horrify the city's dentists.*

above: *An artful display in a Govan fishmonger's window and stained glass on a butcher's shopfront.*

Shopping in Glasgow has always been a popular pursuit. It used to be said that any product made elsewhere in the world was also made in the city. While this is no longer true, you can, by a bizarre post-imperial somersault, buy just about anything in the city – ceramics from Japan, shoes from Italy, apples from Canada, cutlery from Korea – either from the large department stores, dozens of specialist shops or the cosy wee newsagent round the corner.

Department stores selling an assortment of goods under one roof were a Victorian invention. First popular in Paris, many similar emporiums were built in every large city in Europe and North America. Architecturally, they were designed in fashionable styles to impress prospective customers with their elegance and their good taste. Glasgow has an almost perfectly preserved example – Fraser's in Buchanan Street (left).

Fraser's galleried main hall is decorated in a Franco/Italianate style with exuberant plasterwork concealing the cast-iron columns which support the galleries and the graceful, curved iron and glass roof. 'A Commercial Crystal Palace ... a scene of activity and artistic magnificence' was how the Glasgow Herald described the building when it opened. The store also had a steam elevator, possibly the first in the city, and it still has a fairly vintage machine with a wee lady to open and close the concertina gates and press the floor buttons for you.

above: *Fruitshop in Partick.*
left: *The galleried main hall of Fraser's department store.*

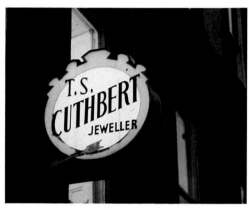

Glasgow's streets are full of delightful serendipity – a bus stop designed to disorientate jet-lagged New Yorkers, stained glass advertising leafy suburbia, shop signs shaped like their products, the TV repairman in Parkhead who's painted his shopfront like a colour test-card, 'the only one in the city, Jimmy', the billiard hall in Mitchell Street where you expect Al Capone to stumble out tommy-gun blazing at the police, having shot up the hall's cavernous interior, the pigeon club in the East End where Glasgow 'hardmen' knowledgably discuss the 'doos', and the polished brass of city law firms and commerce.

The centre of Glasgow today is generally thought to be George Square, or perhaps at the corner of Argyle and Union Streets. In the 18th century the city centre was further east at Glasgow Cross. This area is still the centre of the pre-Victorian city. The Tolbooth Steeple (left) dates from 1626 and the nearby Tron Steeple from 1636. Much of the area around Glasgow Cross was rebuilt in the 19th century when the Glasgow and South Western Railway bulldozed its way to St Enoch Square, but some relics and atmosphere remain from the era of the Tobacco Lords.

Glasgow's early trade was with the American colonies and the West Indies. The city's merchants amassed large fortunes before the American War of Independence temporary halted their activities. By 1775 more than half the tobacco and much of the sugar and rum imported to Britain was landed at Glasgow, to be profitably re-exported to Europe. Many English merchants of the time regretted the Union of 1707 which gave the ambitious Glasgow traders access to what had been their monopoly. The wealth coming into the city from the plantations was used to fund new ventures and to transform the quiet, ecclesiastical, academic market town into a commercial city state. Glasgow took on the mantle of Venice, sending its merchants and seamen to far corners of the globe as the British Empire expanded.

Although the American War of Independence was a setback, Glasgow had already established a manufacturing base and, by the beginning of the 19th century, the city was exporting textiles (the astute merchants had turned to importing cotton after the tobacco trade collapsed), ceramics, carpets and chemicals. Then the mining of large local deposits of coal and iron ore

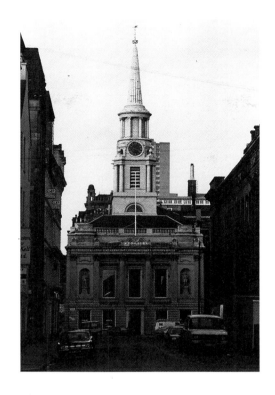

above: *Hutchesons' Hospital (1805) at the end of a typical street vista in the Merchant City, now the Glasgow base of the National Trust for Scotland.*

fuelled the development of the heavy industries and engineering skills for which the city is best known.

The Tobacco Lords and Trades Guilds of the 18th century established commercial attitudes and a civic pride which reached its apogee at the end of the 19th century. Even today city capitalists and councillors talk with a Victorian breadth of vision. Grand civic plans are murmured, big business deals are always in the offing.

The metropolis has had some success in replacing its older industries with micro-electronics, aero-engines and the like. Glasgow is a centre for banking and insurance and is being actively promoted as a conference and tourist centre. And possibly the older industries which have stayed the course – engineering firms and even some shipbuilders – will flourish in the future.

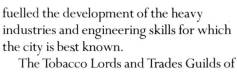

left: *Crown Arcade, originally the Tobacco Exchange in Virginia Street. A late relic of that era, the booth above the pedimented door at the far end is said to have been the auctioneer's box.*

far left: *The Tolbooth Steeple at Glasgow Cross in the mid-19th century.*

North of Glasgow Cross are two of the oldest buildings in the city. The Provand's Lordship was built in 1471 for church envoys visiting the city. It has a plain stone-built exterior with traditional Scottish crow-stepped gables (1670) and inside, some interesting period interiors. Its main distinction, however, is that in a city which has constantly rebuilt itself, the Provand's Lordship still exists today.

Glasgow's Cathedral was constructed over a long period from the late 12th century until the 15th century on a dramatic sloping site. The diocese was originally founded by St Mungo (the city's patron saint) in the 6th century. The present cathedral is one of the oldest and finest Medieval Gothic churches in Scotland. Many others were destroyed during the Reformation, but by some divine salvation perhaps, Glasgow Cathedral survived the depredations of that time. Today, its heavily buttressed exterior retains a majestic, solemn presence in a redeveloped part of the city. Its lofty, silent nave and vaulted lower church provide a meditative escape from the outside world. Suspended in the nave are the regimental colours of many Scottish regiments including the Cameronians, the Highland Light Infantry, the Argyll and Sutherland Highlanders, and there are wall plaques commemorating imperial battles of long ago. The stained glass windows, dozens of them, are a history lesson in themselves. They represent biblical scenes, battle honours, and local trades and industries.

Glasgow's 18th and 19th-century merchants and industrialists must have been a pretty egocentric lot. Not content with having themselves immortalised in stained glass on the Cathedral windows, they built a huge hilltop cemetery for themselves nearby. On top of the hill is the memorial to John Knox, the Catholic who became a Protestant reformer and who surveys the city from atop his pedestal. He is unaware, no doubt, of the religious feuds still enacted on the city's football parks which the memory of his anti-papal crusade has helped perpetuate. Scattered all around him, row upon row as they tumble down the hillside, are the sententious tombstones of Glasgow's commercial aristocracy.

above: *Moonlight over the 'city of the dead'. The tombs display almost every 19th century architectural style visible in the city they overlook.*

left: *The crow-stepped gable of the Provand's Lordship, Glasgow Cathedral, the statue of David Livingstone, and on the skyline, the silhouette of the Necropolis.*

Traditional Glasgow street life is best seen in the Gallowgate/Bridgeton area in the East End. This is a part of the city which has changed most (through industrial decline and demolition) and yet least (having retained its gutsy lack of pretension and community loyalty).

The city's East End was described in 1872 as having '. . . no public monuments . . . a vast area of dwelling-houses, a heavy proportion of which are of the smaller class, and very many of them, the smallest and most wretched'. This description was still true until recently when a comprehensive renewal scheme began to clean the area up. The area's life is most vividly seen in the street markets of Barrowland, 'ra Barras' in local parlance, and Paddy's Market.

Paddy's Market, by the railway arches in Shipbank Lane, was populated in the 19th century by impoverished immigrants. It was Glasgow's old clothes market – for some a profitable trade in recycling, to others a labyrinthian Dickensian underworld. The Barras, east of Glasgow Cross, is the city's largest and most famous street market. It was gradually established by 19th-century street traders who sold odds-and-ends and hand-me-downs obtained from the city's more salubrious neighbourhoods. The first covered market in Barrowland was opened in 1928 and the Barras has since become an institution. However, it is not yet a pastiche of itself, bowdlerised for tourists like London's Covent Garden. The hawkers and traders here still deliver spontaneous lines of witty patter and it is still patronised mainly by local people.

Sometimes it's difficult to tell the traders from their wares. I once saw a lifesize bust of Robert Burns who looked as if he was going to say 'hullo therr'. It's also difficult to believe that all the patter is true. 'Don't be shy tae buy, it's aw good stuff ... see they antlers, ... the last stag shot in Tollcross Park so it is ..' The place is full of comedians. 'Hey Santa, lost yer reindeer?' or to anyone with a camera, 'Err a man wi a camera ... ah hope you're no a spy frae the Social Security, pal' The Barras are also a rich source of bric-à-brac from Glasgow's Victorian and more recent past, and although nobody's yet discovered a Rembrandt hanging in a fusty antique shop, there's always the chance you will.

If you want free entertainment in Glasgow you can watch the street theatre of Barrowland. If you want more conventional performances, then there's a wide choice available in the city. Glasgow is the home of the Scottish National Orchestra, Scottish Opera, Scottish Ballet, the Citizen's Theatre and many other theatrical and musical companies.

Glasgow has an illustrious theatrical history going back to the 16th century when pioneering impressarios ran the gauntlet of church disapproval. Fanatical preachers used to incite mobs to burn theatres in the city, believing them to be the Devil's work, no doubt because they competed for audiences. In the Edwardian era, Glaswegians flocked to theatres and music halls. Many touring companies found Glasgow audiences generous and knowledgeable, but some performers, especially English, recall frightful evenings at the Glasgow Empire. If they fluffed their lines or a joke fell flat, they were dismissed with outrageous cries of 'Away ye go, ya

left: *The Pavilion Theatre, Renfield Street, a traditional pantomime venue.*
below: *The Spanish style Toledo cinema, Muirend.*

monkey!' Visiting comedians often had a hard time, probably because every second Glaswegian is a comic himself. A travelling circus where you could see exotic animals executing improbable tricks, and pantomimes were also popular. They still are every Christmas and New Year.

So too, the cinema. Glasgow in its heyday had over 130 cinemas. It was 'Cinema City', with more picture houses per head of population than anywhere outside the USA. It is not uncommon still, to see long queues trailing around city blocks in the evening rain waiting to see a popular film. Some early cinemas were richly embellished with interior designs borrowed from the music halls they replaced. During the 1920s and 1930s many large new cinemas were built in the city in the Hollywood art deco style of the period. They had marvellous names, evoking the fanciful world projected on their silver screens – Cosmo, Roxy, Astoria, Toledo, Paramount, Rio and Rosevale.

right: *The Theatre Royal, Hope Street, home of Scottish Opera. Its Victorian Rococo decoration dates from 1895.*
below: *Robert Brothers's Circus at the Kelvin Hall.*

Glasgow at night is like a film set from Hollywood's New York in the 1940s. It has its own Broadway (left). It has the same wet, dimly lit, sinister, Chandleresque streets and the cast-iron warehouses. It has the dance halls, the Irish bars and the Italian restaurants. It has the flashing neon signs of Chinese chop-suey joints and loan sharks. And it has its crusading all-night newspapermen with by-lines like 'Voice of the Times' and 'Mr Glasgow', its talkative cabbies, courageous firemen and resourceful police force.

64

There are two types of museum in Glasgow – the People's Palace and all the rest. The People's Palace is unique in Glasgow. It does not attempt to exhibit French Impressionist paintings or Chinese porcelain – the others do this admirably. It records and illustrates the history of Glasgow with particular emphasis on the social life and artefacts of the city's working people.

It was built on Glasgow Green in 1898 and was a 'conscientious effort … to make cultural provision for the city's working classes'. It was hugely popular when first opened. People were entranced by the lush tropical Winter Gardens where they could stroll amongst palm trees and aspidistras and listen to concerts. Redevelopment of the surrounding area recently caused attendances to fall, but people are being encouraged to move back, and the People's Palace should again assume its social significance and historical importance to the city.

Over recent years the museum has built up a large collection of Glaswegiana helped, ironically, by the haste and scale of urban redevelopment. It has an extensive collection of trade union banners, football memorabilia, music hall posters, enamel advertising signs and Victorian stained glass (for which Glasgow was famous). There's even a 1950s jukebox. There are also stories of workers' struggles against high rents and low wages, and of the Bolshevism which swept the shipyards in 1919 earning the city the spurious sobriquet 'Red Clydeside'.

left: *The People's Palace, Glasgow Green.*
bottom left: *Detail of the iron and glass roof of the Winter Gardens.*
top right: *Cast-iron fountain on Glasgow Green.*
right: *Tiled panel made in Glasgow for a fish shop, exhibited in the People's Palace.*

The Glasgow Fair Holiday, the annual trades holiday in the city, dates back to the Middle Ages. Then, it was a boisterous community festival of feasting and entertainment, sideshows and performing animals, held on Glasgow Green. In the late 19th century, the Fair 'went to sea' as families began the tradition of sailing 'doon the watter' to the seaside resorts of Dunoon and Rothesay. Nowadays, they board charter flights to Italy and Spain where the sun seems guaranteed to shine. But there still is a fun-fair held on Glasgow Green during the last two weeks in July.

At the Glasgow Fair you can eat yourself silly with fish and chips, followed by candyfloss . . . discover the concealed curiosities of a 'mini-zoo' . . . win a useless teddy bear playing bingo . . . see if Madame Romney's 'inherited powers' can help you . . . or simply ride on the hobby-horses of a carousel.

This building on Glasgow Green looks as if it could be part of the fun-fair. It's not really, though. It's meant to be the Doge's Palace in Venice. It is Templeton's Carpet Factory and it was built to the design of William Leiper to the wishes of Templetons who hoped 'instead of the ordinary and common factory' to 'erect a building of permanent architectural beauty'.

Well, the result is certainly not ordinary and in a playful way it is quite beautiful.

above and left: *The extraordinary façade of Templeton's Carpet Factory. It is now a business centre inside. Many of Glasgow's Victorian buildings have been converted to other uses while retaining their ornate fronts.*
right: *A 1930s addition to the building continues the style in fine fashion.*

Apparently Templetons asked Leiper what his favourite building was and he replied 'the Doge's Palace'. So that's what Templetons commanded him to build. It was completed in 1889 and its polychrome brickwork and mosaics were viewed with wonderment by the local population. They had never seen anything like it and I doubt if anyone will again. Only the Victorians could seriously build such marvellously absurb decorative follies.

Venetian-style architecture, usually more restrained than the Templeton's example, was popular in Glasgow during the 19th century. Perhaps the city's merchants, industrialists and shipowners liked the association with a renowned maritime civilisation such as Venice, and a number of Glasgow's finer 19th-century buildings follow Venetian patterns. Two of the best are built in cast-iron, a material which was ideal for making repeat patterned, imitation Venetian arches.

The Victorians made great advances in the structural use of iron and steel. They built epic structures like the fabled Crystal Palace in London, Glasgow's Central Station and the Forth Railway Bridge. Indeed, supporting columns concealed behind the stone façades of many Victorian buildings were made of cast-iron. What was unusual in the 1850s was to pre-fabricate a complete building from this material. This is exactly what ironfounder John Baird did in 1855.

Gardner's furniture warehouse in Jamaica Street is Glasgow's most celebrated cast-iron building. It is beautifully

above: *Façade detail on the Ca d'Oro Building, Gordon Street.*
left: *Gardner's Iron Building in Jamaica Street.*
below: *The Clydesdale Bank Building, West George Street.*

proportioned, structurally advanced for its time, immaculately maintained by its original owners and is of great historic architectural importance. Outside America where foundaries in New York mass-produced 'iron-fronts' like Henry Ford built automobiles, Glasgow pioneered this type of building.

Several fine iron buildings like Gardner's still stand today in the city centre. The Ca d'Oro at the corner of Gordon and Union Streets is a more elaborate example. It shows clearly how cast-iron could be moulded to reproduce *en masse* arches, cornices, columns and doorways in complex decorative patterns. The Ca d'Oro was assembled in 1872, yet these early iron buildings were the precursors of the modern steel-framed, glazed office buildings and skyscrapers of today, the better examples of which, like Glasgow's Clydesdale Bank at the corner of Buchanan and West George Streets, manage to achieve the elegant proportions and the deceptively light appearance of their Victorian predecessors.

Ornamental cast-iron work can be found all over the city, on finialled rooflines, balustrades and railings, fountains, park benches and conservatories. Glasgow during the 19th century was a major producer of ornamental cast-iron. Walter MacFarlane's Saracen Foundry at Possilpark and George Smith's Sun Foundry in Parliamentary Road even published illustrated mail-order catalogues of their wares. Much of the production was exported and you can still find Glasgow cast-iron fountains and bandstands as far afield as India and Australia.

Many of the patterns used were borrowed from nature – animals and leaves being thought particularly appropriate for conservatories and parks like the Kibble Palace in Botanic Gardens. The Palace was presented to the city and erected in Botanic Gardens in 1873 by its designer, John Kibble, an engineer and horticulturist who had originally built it on his estate on the shore of Loch Long in 1860. It is a gem among Glasgow's Victorian buildings, a 'Crystal Palace of Art', a 'magnificent hall for music or public speaking' decorated with 'celebrated statuary'.

Its marble statues can still be seen, artfully posed among the sub-tropical plants and cast-iron columns. Glasgow's 19th-century West End plutocrats would perambulate here, sheltered from the weather and serenaded by string quartets – a sensation of genteel pleasure which can still be felt today under the building's graceful glazed domes.

far left: *The dome inside the entrance to the Kibble Palace.*

left: *The main circular arena in the Kibble Palace, showing the cast-iron columns and a statue of a startled Eve.*

below: *Cast-iron squirrels scampering over a park bench in the Botanic Gardens.*

Although more deserve to be better known, only two of Glasgow's many 19th-century architects have received wide recognition outside their city. They are Alexander 'Greek' Thomson and Charles Rennie Mackintosh.

'Greek' Thomson has been called the 'most original architectural designer of the century'. A look at St Vincent Street Church reveals why. St Vincent Street Church (1859) may have started out as a fairly conventional copy of a Greek temple, but raised by Thomson on a giddy series of plinths and pediments on its steeply sloping site, which culminate in a splendidly bizarre Indo/Egyptianesque tower, it has ended up as one of the architectural masterpieces of 19th-century Europe.

At a time when most 'Greek revival' buildings tried to make parts of Edinburgh, for example, look like Athens, Thomson's St Vincent Street Church looks as if it was built for an Indian maharajah rather than the United Presbyterian Church. Thomson's work influenced many other Glasgow architects and several buildings in the city, other than his own churches, warehouses, tenements and terraces, bear the stamp of his style. St Vincent Street Church would stand as a landmark in any great European city. In Glasgow it is also an extraordinary deviation. Most churches in the city at the time were being designed in a range of Gothic styles.

above: *The 19th-century Gothic spires of
Lansdowne Church and St Mary's Cathedral in
Great Western Road.*

left: *'Greek' Thomson's St Vincent Street Church
with (left) the more conventional Gothic spire of
St Columba's Church and (middle distance)
Renfield St Stephen's in Bath Street.*

far left: *Thomsonesque tenements in Nithsdale
Drive.*

Charles Rennie Mackintosh is Glasgow's most celebrated architect and designer. Yet, during his working life he went largely unrecognised in his home city. He was better known on the Continent where his novel architectural and interior designs were appreciated, particularly in Vienna, the avant-garde capital of Europe around 1900.

The Glasgow School of Art, his most famous building, put Glasgow on the international architectural map. It was designed in ineffable style – Scottish art nouveau would be the most approximate description – and constructed in two stages between 1897 and 1909. Mackintosh's remarkably original design for the Art School was considered by some critics to be in gauche bad taste, probably because it didn't look like one of the ersatz Baroque cultural palaces which the Victorians usually liked to build. Today, the Glasgow School of Art is appreciated for what it is – one of the great achievements of early modern architecture.

left: *The library in the Glasgow School of Art, one of Mackintosh's most original interior designs. Mackintosh not only designed the façades of his buildings but almost every detail of the interiors as well – even the furniture and light fittings.*

above: *The west wall of the Art School. The windows shoot up the wall like mini-skyscrapers.*

right: *Mackintosh typography above the entrance to the Glasgow School of Art.*

below: *Art nouveau leaded glass motif in the Glasgow School of Art.*

above: *The entrance to the Art School.*

below: *Studio still life in the Art School.*

above: *The façade of the Willow Tearooms, Sauchiehall Street, and (below) Mackintosh-style lettering advertising the menu.*

Mackintosh's other buildings in Glasgow include the Willow Tearooms in Sauchiehall Street. This building stood empty for some time but it has now been completely restored. On the ground floor are the new premises of a jewellery firm and upstairs there is a re-creation of the original 1904 tearoom. The design was commissioned by Kate Cranston, a well known Glasgow tearoom proprietor who was an enlightened patron of Mackintosh. He designed several

tearoom interiors for her, some in exotic oriental styles, of which the Willow Tearooms is the only survivor.

Glasgow at the turn of the century, like Paris, Brussels, Vienna and Barcelona, experienced a flowering of the art nouveau style, mainly due to Mackintosh's influence. Several city buildings remain as evidence of this and many tenement closes are still adorned with art nouveau decorative tiles.

above: *Shop window display of reproduction Mackintosh furniture made in Italy.*
below: *Art nouveau wood façade (c1900) on the Roost Bar (now the Exchequer) in Dumbarton Road and (left) the doorway of the Savings Bank of Glasgow in Anderston, of the same period.*

Although Glasgow is pre-eminently a Victorian city, it also contains buildings of the art deco period of the 1920s and 1930s. Cinemas are the most obvious of these, but there are also art deco office blocks, shopfronts, bar and café fascias. Unlike the Victorian buildings, these art deco works have yet to acquire the patina of time which will once again make them fashionable, although there are signs that this is beginning to happen.

top right: *Art deco façade on a Partick bar in Dumbarton Road.*
above: *The 1930s façade of the Beresford Hotel, Sauchiehall Street.*
right: *Art deco sign and window patterns on the Rosevale Bar, Partick.*
far right: *The Rubaiyat, Byres Road, with a doorway looking like the panelling and portholes on a 1930s steamship.*

You wouldn't think it, considering Glasgow's reputation for having a hard drinking population, but the city did have a strong temperance movement in Victorian/Edwardian times. They preached the virtues of abstinence and of the vices of the 'demon drink'. These teetotallers denounced the debauchery of Glasgow Saturday nights, but were opposed by equally fanatical drinkers. Some Clyde paddle steamers in those days were 'dry ships' while others (to escape the restrictions of licensing laws) were loaded to the gunnels with cheap whisky. The Glasgow expression 'steaming' (drunk) has its origin here. Nobody came back sober after a sail on one of these floating gin-palaces.

Pub landlords did not consider the temperance men and women their favourite people. To encourage respectable customers and to elevate their own reputations, they commissioned expensive interior designs for their bars. These late 19th-century 'oases

left: *The stunning 1880s opulence inside the Horsehoe Bar, Drury Street.*
below: *'Take a photy o'him . . . he's ma pal, so he is.' Two punters in Brechin's Bar, Govan.*

of refreshment' boasted interiors of sumptuous, stunning opulence. They were characterised by huge carved mahogany or walnut bars, stained glass, massive framed gilt mirrors from floor to ceiling, marble tables, brass light-fittings, decorative tilework, polished wood panelling and imitation plasterwork ceilings held up by cast-iron Corinthian columns. Fluctuating fashions have seen many of these extravagantly decorated bars altered or, in one notable case, dismantled and shipped to America, but fortunately a few splendid examples survive in the city.

top left: *The immaculate typography on the façade of the Horseshoe Bar.*
above: *Ornamental blacksmith in the Horseshoe Bar. The bar was apparently built on the site of an old stable.*
left: *Ornate Victorian advertising mirrors in the Old Toll Bar (1892) in Paisley Road.*

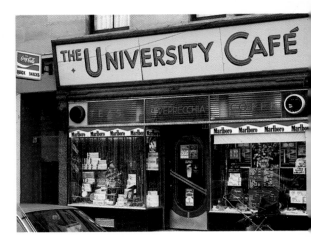

For those who prefer to avoid the esoteric, aggressively masculine environment of Glasgow's bars, there are many cafés, tearooms and cocktail bars in the city. The cocktail bars are a fairly recent and trendy feature, while the tearooms, where you can 'gossip happily while admiring the hats at the next table' are almost a city institution. Glasgow café society too has its traditions, whether catering for shipyard workers, art students at the Third Eye Centre or simply those in search of a decent cup of coffee. You can usually find one in the many Italian cafés in the city. You can also sample their delicious ice cream, specially sweetened, it seems for the Glasgow sweet tooth, or admire their 1930s glass and chrome fascias.

top left: *The Cafe Gandolfi, Albion Street. The Gandolfi was the first and remains the best of Glasgow's recent continental café/bars.*
left: *De Quincy's, Renfield Street. Its walls, ceilings and arches are adorned with turn of the century Moorish tilework, once part of an insurance office.*
above: *Kings Café, Elmbank Street.*
right: *Central Café, Saltmarket, Queens Café, Victoria Road, University Café, Byres Road and Hubbard's, Great Western Road.*

84

The Italians, who began coming to Scotland in the 19th century, are not alone among immigrants to Glasgow. The city's culture and accent are so ethnic in themselves that Glasgow will never become cosmopolitan in an amorphous way – the Italians who return to their Tuscan hill towns speak to the locals with a Glasgow accent. But the city is open to influences from abroad. Glaswegians have acquired a taste for Italian ice cream, Pakistani and Indian curries and Chinese concoctions from Hong Kong.

When Glasgow Corporation sent a recruiting team to the Punjab in the 1950s to bring back bus conductors, they probably didn't expect to get the food as well. But most Glaswegians are glad they did. After the bars closed, fish and chips wrapped in newspapers was the only 'carry-out' you could eat before then. There's nothing wrong with fish and chips, but it's nice nowadays to have a choice. Other people from overseas have enriched Glasgow's life. The city has a sizable and long established Jewish population and even a small Polish community. However, its most prominent minorities came from Ireland and the Scottish Highlands during the 19th century, and most Glaswegians today can claim some ancestry from these 'huddled masses'.

far left: *Fazzi Brothers Italian delicatessen in Cambridge Street, Chinese restaurant in Sauchiehall Street and supermarket staff in Cambridge Street.*
above: *Grocer in Albert Drive.*
left: *Schoolchildren, Hillhead.*
below: *Indian restaurant, Gibson Street.*

Eastern cultures not only tempt the city's palate but also decorate the streets. Brightly coloured saris swish by in front of grocers selling coriander and chillies. There's even an oriental gable-end painting in Woodside. Beneath the painting immigrant children, adopting local customs, play football.

Football is a religion in Glasgow – in more ways than one. The traditional Celtic v Rangers fixture, the 'Old Firm', is an excuse to act out old Catholic v Protestant antipathies as much as it's a popular sporting event. Glasgow is the home of the Scottish Football League. The city's Queens Park Football Club dates from 1867 and their Hampden Park is the national stadium for Scotland. Many other sports are played in Glasgow. Cricket has been played in the

city since the late 18th century. Rugby and golf are popular and the city boasts one of the biggest entries in the world for its marathon. Whether they all finish is another matter. There's even an ice-hockey team. But football is by far the most popular and it retains its zealous following. Clyde FC and Partick Thistle are the city's other league clubs and both have loyal support from their fans. 'Thistle' have a notably eccentric following. The team, always the underdogs, has a celebrated if unfair reputation for losing.

below: *'Football retains its zealous support':
Rangers fans at Ibrox Park.*

left: *Oriental gable-end mural in Woodside and a
European sculptured companion piece at St
George's Cross.*

above: *The glazed courtyard leading off the entrance hall.*
below: *'Jockeys in the Rain' by Degas, one aspect of Burrell's extensive collection.*
right: *'The Thinkers'.*

Not all Glaswegians or visitors to the city want to spend their time at football games or in bars, although I can recommend some of the latter. The city's museums and art galleries are hugely popular – and they are free.

The Burrell Collection is among the newest museums in the city, although its exhibits include some of rare antiquity. The collection, noted for its 19th-century French paintings, oriental ceramics and prints, medieval stained glass and tapestries, belonged to wealthy 19th-century Glasgow shipowner, Sir William Burrell, and it was gifted to the city in 1944. After years of storage and temporary exhibition, it was finally housed in a purpose-built modern building opened in 1983.

Burrell was an astute businessman. He made his fortune in his early years and was able to devote his later life exclusively to his passion – collecting *objets d'art*. He was a frequent visitor to the antique salerooms of Europe. He made annual trips to Paris and even ventured to the Far East in pursuit of his expensive hobby. In later life he lived a reclusive, eccentric existence in his Gothic castle in Berwickshire, surrounded by his treasures – a Scottish *Citizen Kane*. Burrell loved a bargain, and it is surprising that such a collection, world class in its range and quality, could be amassed by a man who apparently hated to part with his money. Parsimonious as he may have been, he was a perspicacious buyer. Many of the 8000 items in this extraordinary collection are the envy of museums throughout the world.

right: *A spotlit life-size Buddha leads the eye to the wooded parkland beyond the gallery. The exciting modern building which houses Burrell's treasures is as distinguished as the collection itself. It is set in the sylvan surroundings of Pollok Park three miles from the city centre.*

Glasgow's other major municipal museum is the Art Gallery and Museum at Kelvingrove. The building, in complete contrast to the Burrell, is the sort of megalomaniacal edifice which the late Victorians delighted in designing. It is an extraordinary *mélange* of towers and cupolas. Its façade is clumsily cluttered with mock-Renaissance details, but from a distance its romantic roofline captures the confidence and the spirit of its time.

The Art Galleries were built for the 1901 International Exhibition – a typically Victorian jamboree where the latest products of the industrialised world were put on show. Inside, the building's lofty interior contains the finest civic art collection in Britain. Among the exhibits are a superb group of French Impressionists, paintings by Rembrandt and Dali, European ceramics and jewellery, a fine collection of arms and armour, an excellent group of Scottish paintings, and furniture by Charles Rennie Mackintosh.

above: *Looking like winter in Vienna, Glasgow Art Gallery as seen from Park Terrace.*
left: *'Ah'm just making sure it's no a photy':*
Visitor inspecting a Signac in the French Impressionist room.
right: *Equestrian exhibit in the arms and armour gallery and ceiling detail in the main gallery.*

Another fine city gallery can be found at Glasgow University, which overlooks Kelvingrove Park. Housed in a modern building on the University's campus is the Hunterian Art Gallery. It is renowned for its collection of Scottish paintings, unrivalled examples of Whistler's work and an award-winning reconstruction of Charles Rennie Mackintosh's Glasgow residence, decorated with the great man's work.

Glaswegians are among the most educated citizens in Britain. Their sometimes incoherent speech may not make this seem credible, but it's not uncommon to meet some wee guy in a bar who's just read *War and Peace* or a similar literary epic. By the 1850s most children in the city were attending school, and the Andersonian Institution, founded in 1795 and now Strathclyde University, was a pioneering technical college. Glasgow University itself was founded as long ago as 1451, and the city has a tradition of broadly based liberal education. The Mitchell Library is one of the largest reference libraries in Europe and its reading rooms are always full of people researching academic or personal projects.

Glasgow University's Victorian Gothic building was designed by Sir George Gilbert Scott and built between 1866 and 1887. Scott, despite his name, was an Englishman. He must have been influenced by the spires and crow-stepped gables of Scottish baronial chateaux and assumed that his Franco/Scottish Gothic design would be appropriate to a Glasgow setting. In a symbolic way the spires and tower are. From their hilltop, they point heavenwards on the path of truth, wisdom and enlightenment, to the sure destination of all worthy educated Victorians.

above: *John Smith's bookshop in St Vincent Street. Smith's, Scotland's oldest and most distinguished bookshop, is a favourite haunt of Glasgow book lovers and students (it has a branch on Gilmorehill).*

left: *The twilight silhouette of Glasgow University on Gilmorehill.*
right: *The University tower seen from the River Clyde.*

'The Clyde made Glasgow, and Glasgow made the Clyde.' Clichés, no matter how debased, usually contain some lasting truth. This one is no exception. Embraced by these nine memorable words are the remarkable achievements of this proud, hard-bitten, optimistic, noble city, and of its friendly people.

The silent, eternal waters of the River Clyde.

95

Glasgow nocturne, Govan Shipbuilders.

Picture credits: *All photographs are by Robin Ward except as follows:* Page 4 T & R Annan and Sons, Glasgow. Page 22 (top) Strathclyde Regional Archives, (bottom) T & R Annan and Sons. Page 23 (top and bottom) T & R Annan and Sons. Page 32 (top) T & R Annan and Sons. Page 33 Strathclyde Regional Archives. Page 36 and 37 (bottom) University of Glasgow/Scottish Record Office. Page 38 and 39 Mitchell Library, Glasgow. Page 54 Mitchell Library.

Special thanks is due to Glasgow Museums and Art Galleries for permission to photograph their collections, and to the many people and institutions in the city who were helpful in the preparation of this book.